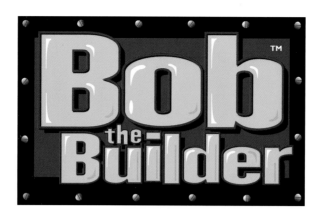

Bob the Builder

Celebration Cakes

13 fun cake projects featuring Bob and his team

HiT entertainment

by Jan Clement-May

First published in March 2007 by B. Dutton Publishing Limited, Alfred House, Hones Business Park, Farnham, Surrey, GU9 8BB, UK.

ISBN-13: 978-905113-05-7

Text and cake design: Jan Clement-May

Typography and photography: B. Dutton Publishing Limited.

Publisher: Beverley Dutton

Editor: Jenny Stewart

Sub Editor: Clare Porter

Designer: Sarah Richardson

Design Assistant: Zena Manicom

Photography: Alister Thorpe

Cover Image: Rob Goves

Printed in Slovenia by arrangement with Associated Agencies Limited

Models: Blake, Flora, Matthew and Oliver

Dedication

This book is dedicated to my husband, Ian, and children, Emelia and Christian. Thank you for your patience and putting up with all the mess and chaos created throughout the house whilst all my efforts where being channelled into creating this book.

Acknowledgements

I would like to give a special thank you to Beverley and Rob for giving me the opportunity and having faith in me to design and create cakes.

Thanks also to Alister for his superb photography; Sarah and Jenny for their support, guidance and endless humour; and Daisy at HIT Entertainment for her inspiration.

Introduction

Bob the Builder first came to my attention when my children were quite small – we would regularly watch him and his friends in different adventures on the television and videos, over and over again. As my children grew older, I became out of touch with Bob and had no idea that he had become eco-friendly, had moved to Sunflower Valley and even gone to the Wild West!

When I was given the opportunity to recreate Bob in sugar for a collection of cake designs my pencil ran riot on the paper! I got carried away with the colours, sets and formats in which Bob and his friends could be portrayed, and all the exciting new characters gave me a great deal of inspiration for fun designs. Sadly, there wasn't enough room to fit them all in this book, so I narrowed it down to a collection of cakes that offer something for everyone. If you are a beginner, there are several simple projects that are easy to achieve; if you are an experienced sugarcrafter looking for a challenge, you will find more involved designs to inspire you. I also added a couple of 'quick cakes', simple adaptations of projects that are perfect if you're short of time!

I hope you enjoy sitting with the children and looking through the pages within, picking out a birthday cake adorned with a favourite character to take pride of place on the party table, or even a special Christmas cake with a cheeky twist. Whatever the occasion and whichever project you choose to attempt, I hope that you have great pleasure in making your own cake and enjoy the compliments that are sure to follow when your masterpiece is the centre of attention!

Jan
x

Jan Clement-May

Contents

RECIPES

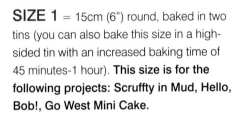

Sponge cake

The ingredients for all the cakes are virtually the same, but you will need to adjust the quantities and baking time according to the size of the cake, as shown in the table below.

SIZE 1 = 15cm (6") round, baked in two tins (you can also bake this size in a high-sided tin with an increased baking time of 45 minutes-1 hour). **This size is for the following projects: Scruffty in Mud, Hello, Bob!, Go West Mini Cake.**

SIZE 2 = 20.5cm (8") square or round, baked in two tins (you can also bake this size in a high-sided tin with an increased baking time of 1-1¼ hours); 16.5cm (6½") sphere; 23cm x 30.5cm (9" x 12") rectangle. **This size is for the following projects: Scrambler and Scruffty's Muddy Adventure!, Off to Work!, Bob's Toolbox, Muck Gets Mucky!*, Building in Progress, Stinky Spud and Wild Patch Go West!, Spud's Halloween Pumpkin, Caught in a Snowball, Spud's Secret Christmas Present Surprise!.**

*Trim 13cm (5") off the end off the rectangle to achieve the required size for Muck.

CUPCAKES: bake as many batches of 12 cupcakes as required for the **Cupcakes from Bobsville**. (I baked 52 cupcakes for the display, i.e. five batches with some spare cakes.)

INGREDIENTS	SIZE 1	SIZE 2	CUPCAKES
Soft margarine	175g (6oz)	225g (8oz)	100g (4oz)
Caster sugar	175g (6oz)	225g (8oz)	100g (4oz)
Baking powder	8ml (1½tsp)	10ml (2tsp)	5ml (1tsp)
Self-raising flour	225g (8oz)	275g (10oz)	100g (4oz)
Eggs	3	5	2
Milk	23ml (1½tbsp)	30ml (2tbsp)	N/A
BAKING TIME	30 minutes	40 minutes/ 50 minutes for the spherical cake	18-20 minutes

Sponge cake method: round, square and rectangular

1 Preheat the oven to 180°C/350°F/gas mark 4. Grease the baking tin/s and line the base with greaseproof paper or baking parchment. Cut a length of greaseproof paper or baking parchment to fit all the way around the inside of the tin/s. For the rectangular cake, grease and line a baking tray.

2 Place all the ingredients into a mixing bowl and beat together in a mixer for approximately 2 minutes (or by hand) until well blended. Pour the mixture into the prepared tin/s and level the top.

3 Bake in the preheated oven for the specified time, or until the cake is firm to the touch and the cake has shrunk away from the sides of the tin. Leave to cool in the tin/s before turning out onto a cooling rack.

Sponge cake method: spherical

1 Preheat the oven to 180°C/350°F/gas mark 4. Grease and flour both halves of the mould.

2 Place all the ingredients into a mixing bowl and beat together in a mixer for approximately 2 minutes (or by hand) until well blended. Fill the lower half of the mould with the mixture and assemble the mould into the stand. Bake for approximately 50 minutes, turning after 35 minutes. To rotate the mould, release the wire clip and turn the sphere on the stand so that the air hole in the tin is pointing downwards.

3 When baked, remove the mould from the oven and allow to stand until slightly cooled. Remove the top half of the mould and leave to cool completely before removing from the lower half of the mould.

Cupcake method

1 Preheat the oven to 200°C/400°F/gas mark 6. Place paper cases into a 12-hole bun tin.

2 Place all the ingredients into a mixing bowl and beat together in a mixer for approximately 2 minutes (or by hand) until well blended. Half-fill the paper cases with the cake mixture and level the tops.

3 Bake in the preheated oven for around 18-20 minutes, or until the cakes have risen and are firm to the touch. Remove the cakes from the bun tin and leave to cool on a cooling rack.

Variations

There are several ways to add flavour to the basic sponge cake recipe.

Chocolate sponge: add (3 tbsp) of good quality cocoa powder mixed with 60ml (4tbsp) of hot water. Allow to cool before adding to the cake mixture.

Lemon sponge: add the rind of 2 lemons and 60ml (4tbsp) of juice from the lemons to the cake mixture.

Orange sponge: add the rind of 2 oranges and 60ml (4tbsp) of juice from the oranges to the cake mixture.

Coffee sponge: add 30ml (2tbsp) of coffee essence to the cake mixture.

Buttercream

INGREDIENTS

175g (6oz) margarine or unsalted butter, softened
450g (1lb) icing sugar, sifted
10ml (2tsp) milk
5ml (1tsp) vanilla essence

Makes around 625g (1lb 6oz) of buttercream

Method

1 Put the margarine or butter in a mixer and beat until it appears lighter in colour. Add the vanilla essence and sifted icing sugar, a little at a time. Blend all the icing sugar and milk gradually until it becomes a light and fluffy mix.

2 To store, place in an airtight container and refrigerate. Use within 10 days. Bring to room temperature and mix again before use.

Variations

There are several ways to add flavour to the basic buttercream recipe.

Chocolate buttercream: add 45ml (3tbsp) of cocoa to the icing sugar and sift before blending.

Lemon or orange buttercream: add 45ml (3tbsp) of lemon or orange curd when blending the buttercream together.

Coffee buttercream: add 30-45ml (2-3tbsp) of coffee essence into the mixer when blending.

Before you start, it is important to ensure that you have the necessary equipment required to create the cake projects. This list is essentially the basic 'tool kit' required throughout the book for covering and decorating the cakes; additional items are included in the list given at the beginning of each project. You can find all the equipment you will need in sugarcraft shops (see page 80 for a full list of suppliers).

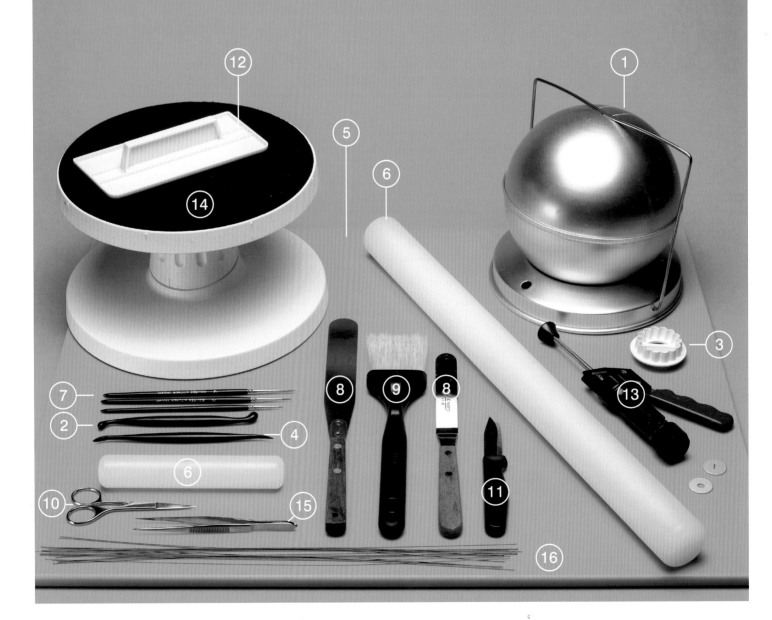

1. Bakeware

Good quality bakeware is essential for successful baking. Most of the projects in this book use three basic cake shapes, i.e. round, square or spherical, so check the size in the Materials list before baking the cake. The quantity of cake mix and buttercream required is given on pages 6 to 7.

2. Bone tool/ball tool

A bone tool or ball tool is particularly useful for figure modelling and can be used to add texture to a covered cake or board. Both ends are used to make indentations or hollows in paste, e.g. to create eye sockets.

3. Cutters

It is always useful to have a selection of cutters to hand for making shapes quickly and easily; specific cutters are listed with each project. A carnation cutter is perfect for making the sunflowers from Sunflower Valley.

4. Dresden tool

This tool is absolutely essential for Sugar Dough modelling. It is an extremely versatile tool as it can be used to mark and texture the paste to create different effects, e.g. the creases in Bob's overalls.

5. Non-stick board

A large, non-stick, polythene board is useful for rolling out Sugar Dough as it is smooth, easy to clean and mobile. Alternatively, you can use a clean work surface.

6. Non-stick rolling pins

You will need a large, non-stick rolling pin to roll out large quantities of Sugar Dough for covering cakes and boards. A small rolling pin is also useful when making smaller items.

7. Paintbrushes

Good quality brushes are used for painting onto Sugar Dough and for applying edible sugar glue. It is useful to have medium, small and fine brushes to hand.

8. Palette knife

Large and small palette knives are ideal for moving covered cakes and small Sugar Dough pieces. You can slide the knife under the cake/paste to avoid marking the surface and distorting the shape.

9. Pastry brush

A pastry brush can be used for brushing cooled, boiled water onto the cake drum to help the Sugar Dough stick.

10. Scissors

A small pair of sharp scissors is invaluable for sugar modelling: keep a pair solely for sugarcraft use.

11. Sharp knife

A sharp will cut through Sugar Dough cleanly, giving a neat edge to sugar pieces and cake/board coverings.

12. Smoother

A smoother is required to give a smooth, professional finish to the covered cake and cake drum.

13. Sugar shaper

A sugar shaper is supplied with several discs, each of which produces a different effect, e.g. a rope or ribbon. Sugar Dough should be softened with a little white vegetable fat before it is extruded through a sugar shaper to ensure the paste comes out smoothly.

14. Turntable

A turntable is very useful when covering and decorating cakes as it allows you to work on the cake without having to handle it too much. Whilst it is possible to work without a turntable, it is useful to have if you decorate cakes on a regular basis.

15. Tweezers

It is handy to have a pair of tweezers when handling tiny pieces such as wires.

16. Wires

Floristry wires are available in various gauges and colours. They have been used to add support to sugar pieces, e.g. Bird's legs, and for the stems of the sunflowers. It is important to remember that wires should never be inserted directly into a cake and any wired items must be safely removed before the cake is eaten.

EDIBLE MATERIALS

There is a huge range of edible pastes, colours and ingredients designed specifically for cake decorating. Always ensure that the materials you use are food-grade (i.e. completely safe to eat). The following list covers most of the edibles you will need for the projects in this book, all of which are available from food decoration specialists Squires Kitchen, or sugarcraft shops (see page 80 for a full list of suppliers).

Clear piping gel

This edible gel is perfect for creating water effects on cakes and is ready-to-use from the pot. Depending on the effect you are aiming to achieve, it can be applied with a paintbrush or piping bag.

Confectioners' glaze

To give sugar models a shiny finish and to seal dust colours, you can varnish them with edible confectioners' glaze. Apply with a paintbrush and clean the brush after use with glaze cleaner (isopropyl alcohol).

Edible glue

This is a clear sugar glue that is used to secure Sugar Dough pieces together. Use a fine paintbrush to apply the glue and be careful not to use too much as this will cause the Sugar Dough to become slippery. See also Working with Sugar Dough, pages 11 to 12.

Dust food colours

There is a huge range of regular edible dust colours, plus pastel, lustrous, iridescent, glitter and sparkle-effect colours, so there is a great deal of scope for creating different

effects on your sugar work. Dust colours can also be mixed with a little clear alcohol, such as vodka or gin, to make a quick-drying paint, or cooled, boiled water.

Edible metallic paint

Pre-mixed edible gold and silver paint is ideal for creating a metallic effect on items such as belt buckles and metal tools. Apply with a paintbrush and clean the brush after use with glaze cleaner (isopropyl alcohol).

Food colour pens

These pens are ideal for beginners as they are easy to use on sugar work. They can be used to write inscriptions on cakes, add fine detail, and are perfect for drawing the outline on the animated grass pieces that can be seen in Sunflower Valley!

Organic chocolate

If you need to create mud on a cake, melted chocolate is perfect! I always use a good quality couverture chocolate as it

tastes delicious and gives good texture to the cake design. Children will love helping out with 'muddy' cake projects!

Paste food colours

There is a vast range of food colours available, allowing you to make almost any colour you require. Paste colours are primarily used to colour Sugar Dough and other sugar pastes, and can also be painted onto sugar models. For more information on using paste food colours, see page 11.

SK Sugar Dough

Sugar Dough is a wonderful modelling medium that can also be used as a cake covering. It is available in 12 ready-made colours plus white and can also be coloured with paste food colours. Sugar Dough dries firm so it holds its shape, but still remains soft enough to eat. For more information, see Working with Sugar Dough, pages 11 to 12.

WORKING with SUGAR DOUGH

SK Sugar Dough is a smooth, non-sticky paste that lends itself perfectly to figure modelling and can also be used as a cake covering. It is available in the following ready-made colours: Black, Blue, Brown, Flesh, Golden Bear Brown, Green, Maroon, Orange, Peach, Red, Violet, White and Yellow.

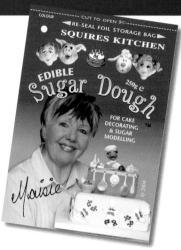

Kneading and softening

It is important to knead Sugar Dough well before use to ensure it is soft and pliable. Rub a little white vegetable fat into your hands to prevent the paste from sticking, then knead the Sugar Dough until soft and smooth. The paste is now ready to use.

If you are using a sugar shaper, you will need to add a little white vegetable fat to the Sugar Dough to soften the paste, making it easier to extrude through the disc.

Drying

Sugar Dough will dry firm if left for several hours, so make sure you allow plenty of time for drying, particularly when making supporting pieces and upright figures. When making rounded shapes, such as heads, allow to dry upside down on a food-grade foam pad to prevent the paste from cracking or becoming flat. When making thin pieces, such as the Christmas tree sections in Spud's Secret Christmas Present Surprise!, handle them carefully as they may break easily.

Supports

Some Sugar Dough pieces may need some extra support, so you can use pieces of raw, dried spaghetti pushed into the paste. Alternatively, you can make your own sugar sticks by rolling short lengths of Sugar Dough (or extruding them through a sugar shaper with a medium hole disc if you have one). Leave to dry completely on a food-grade foam pad for 24 hours and store in an airtight container.

For thinner items, such as Bird's legs, use floristry wire (available from sugarcraft shops). Where a thicker support is required, you can use the candy sticks that are available from confectionery shops.

Whilst some of these supports are edible, they are very hard and can be a choking hazard, so always remember to safely remove any items with internal supports before the cake is eaten.

Colouring

In order to achieve realistic colours for Bob and his friends, you may have to add paste or dust colours to the existing Sugar Dough range.

Paste food colours should be added to the Sugar Dough a tiny amount at a time using the end of a cocktail stick or similar. Knead the Sugar Dough well to ensure the colour is blended in and continue adding and kneading until the required colour is achieved. If too much colour is added, knead some White Sugar Dough into the paste to make it paler. Always colour slightly more than required as it

can be difficult to match the colour exactly if you run out and need to make more.

You can also use paste food colours to paint detail on the surface of your work. Dilute with cooled, boiled water or clear alcohol, such as vodka or gin, and paint onto the Sugar Dough using a paintbrush. Try not to get the Sugar Dough too wet as it will start to dissolve.

TIP

Some food colour pastes are strong and can stain your hands when kneading. To prevent this, rub some white vegetable fat into your hands beforehand and wash them straight afterwards with warm, soapy water. Alternatively, you may prefer to wear food-grade, plastic gloves.

Dust food colours can be brushed onto whole items to alter the colour, or can be used to enhance pieces of work. In addition to the huge range of regular colours, there are pastel, lustrous, iridescent, glitter and sparkle-effect ranges that can be used to create many different effects. To use, sprinkle a little dust onto a piece of kitchen towel, pick up the colour on a paintbrush, tap the brush to remove any excess dust, then brush the colour onto the surface of the Sugar Dough. If a stronger colour is required, simply add more layers of dust or make a paint by mixing the dust colour with a little clear alcohol, such as vodka or gin, or cooled, boiled water in a palette. The alcohol or water will evaporate to leave the colour on the surface (alcohol will evaporate much more quickly). Once the paint has dried in the palette, you can add more alcohol/water to bring it back to a painting consistency.

TIP

You can change the colour of the characters' clothes to suit different designs and seasons, as shown in Spud's various costumes. To change Wendy from her skiwear into her work clothes, simply change the colours and accessories to make them more like Bob's.

Storing

After you have opened a packet of Sugar Dough, it is essential to keep the remaining paste airtight, otherwise it will dry out and become unusable. Open packets of paste can be resealed at the top, placed in a resealable food-grade plastic bag with the air pushed out and stored in an airtight container at room temperature. If you have any spare Sugar Dough that has been coloured, wrap it well in a double layer of cling film, then place in a resealable food-grade plastic bag in an airtight container.

Sugar Dough can be frozen if wrapped well and should be allowed to defrost thoroughly before use.

TECHNIQUES

Carving and shaping a cake

If the cake needs to be stacked and carved to the required shape, such as in Off to Work!, place the sponge cakes on top of each other with a thin layer of buttercream between each one. Using a large, serrated carving knife, carefully shape the cake from the top downwards.

Once the cake is the required shape, spread a thin layer of buttercream over the carved surface and place in the fridge until cold (this gives a smoother surface). In some cases, such as Bob's Toolbox, the cake is cut to shape before the pieces are stacked; again, apply a thin layer of buttercream between the pieces and on any cut surfaces.

Crumb-coating a cake

If you are using a shaped cake, spread a second layer of buttercream over the whole surface area of the cake to seal it and place in the refrigerator to firm. For cakes that require no shaping, sandwich with buttercream, then seal with a layer of buttercream and refrigerate. The buttercream surface should be firm, giving a smooth surface to work on.

Covering a cake

Spread a little buttercream on the cake base to hold the cake in place and position it on the cake drum.

Knead and soften the required quantity of Sugar Dough to cover the cake. Dust a non-stick board with icing sugar to prevent the paste from sticking and roll out the paste, rotating it regularly, until it is large enough to cover the whole cake (top and sides). The paste should be approximately 5mm ($^1/_8$") thick.

Loosely fold the Sugar Dough over the rolling pin, carefully lift it and place it over the cake. Ease the paste down the sides of the cake using the palm of your hand, taking care not to pull the paste downwards as it may crack and tear.

Smooth over the top and sides of the cake with a smoother and cut away any excess paste at the base of the cake with a sharp knife. Smooth around the base of the cake for a neat finish.

Covering a cake drum

Depending on which design you are making, there are two different methods of covering a cake drum (also known as a cake board).

Method 1: To cover a cake drum completely, first dampen the cake drum with cooled, boiled water using a pastry brush. Roll out the required amount of Sugar Dough on a non-stick board dusted with icing sugar. Position the Sugar Dough over the cake drum, smooth over with a smoother and run a sharp knife around the edge of the cake drum to trim away any excess paste. Run your finger around the cut edge to smooth it down. Cover the cake separately on a spare board and place it in position on the covered drum.

Method 2: To cover the outer area of the cake drum around the base of the covered cake, dampen the exposed cake drum with cooled, boiled water using a pastry brush. Roll out a long strip of Sugar Dough, at least as long as the circumference of the cake and as wide as the exposed drum. Cut a straight edge along one side with a sharp knife and secure the strip to the cake drum with the straight edge against the base of the cake. Cut to size and run a smoother over the surface to hide any joins. Cut away excess paste from the edge of the cake drum with a sharp knife and smooth over the cut edge with your finger, as in Method 1.

Trimming with ribbon

To add a finishing touch to a cake design, secure a 1.5cm width ribbon to the edge of the cake drum to match or complement the colour of the cake. Use a non-toxic glue stick to secure the ribbon in place, being very careful to ensure that the glue does not to come into contact with the Sugar Dough. Attach the ribbon carefully and evenly, starting at the back of the cake. Cut to size, allowing a little overlap, and secure neatly with the non-toxic glue stick.

Scrambler and Scruffty's Muddy Adventure!

Materials

20.5cm (8") round sponge cake
450g (1lb) buttercream
SK Sugar Dough: 400g (14oz) Black, 350g (12¼oz) Blue, 10g (¼oz) Brown, 750g (1lb 10½oz) Green, 180g (6¼oz) White
250g (8¾oz) SK Organic Milk Chocolate Couverture
SK Food Colour Pen: Holly/Ivy
SK Dust Food Colours: Daffodil, Shady Moss
SK Magic Sparkles
SK Edible Paint: Gold and Silver
SK Edible Glue
SK Confectioners' Glaze
Icing sugar in sugar shaker
Cooled, boiled water
White vegetable fat

Equipment

30.5cm (12") round cake drum
100cm (39") x 1.5cm (½") width ribbon: blue
Non-toxic glue stick
Non-stick board and rolling pin
2 x 5cm (2") lengths 26-gauge floristry wire: white
Ball tool
Embroidery grid embosser (PC)
Geometrical cutter set (FMM)
Paintbrushes: small, medium and flat
Scissors
Short length thin dowelling (e.g. barbeque skewer)
Small pieces food-grade foam sponge for support
Small, sharp knife
Small spoon
Smoother
Sugar shaper
Templates (see page 79)

For the materials, equipment and instructions required to make Scruffty, see pages 20 to 21.

METHOD

Preparing the grass

1 Roll out 150g (5¼oz) of Green Sugar Dough and cut three of each of the grass templates A and B. Set aside to dry.

Covering the cake

2 Cut and fill the sponge cake with buttercream, then position the cake centrally on the cake drum. Cover the cake with a thin layer of buttercream to help the Sugar Dough stick to the cake.

3 Roll out 600g (1lb 5¼oz) of Green Sugar Dough on a non-stick board dusted with icing sugar and cover the cake. Smooth over the top and sides with a smoother and cut away any excess at the base of the cake with a sharp knife.

4 Knead together the trimmings of Green Sugar Dough and roll out a strip long enough to fit all the way around the cake base. Cut a straight edge on one side of the strip, dampen the cake drum with cooled, boiled water and fix the strip to the cake drum. Cut to size and smooth down the joins, then trim off any excess paste from around the edge of the cake drum using a sharp knife.

Scrambler

5 Knead 10g (¼oz) of White Sugar Dough and soften with a little white vegetable fat. Push through a sugar shaper with a round hole disc to make the front grille, back seat and the back shelf section, as shown. Set aside to dry and support the front grille section in a curved position with small foam pieces.

6 Roll out 160g (5½oz) of Black Sugar Dough to a thickness of 1.5cm (½"), cut out a rectangle measuring 5cm x 10cm (2" x 4") and secure to the centre of the cake top.

7 Roll out 180g (6¼oz) of Blue Sugar Dough slightly thicker than the black base and cut to the same size. Roll out 40g (1½oz) of Blue Sugar Dough to 1cm (¼") thick for the back plate under the seat and cut off the front corners, as shown.

8 Roll out 40g (1½oz) of Blue Sugar Dough and cut four arches using templates C and D (cut two of each). Set aside to dry in an arched position, ensuring the edge is straight. Make sure that you have opposite shapes to fit on either side.

9 Model a triangular shape for the front panel from 70g (2½oz) of Blue Sugar Dough and round off the corners. Divide 10g (¼oz) of Blue Sugar Dough in half and shape into cones for the eyes. Shape 5g (just under ¼oz) of paste for the handlebar base and push a short length of dowelling into the base to give support when attached.

10 Roll out 5g (just under ¼oz) of Blue Sugar Dough and cut two circles using the no. 3 cutter from the geometrical set. Cut each one into two, then mark an inner line in each with the cutter, making sure you do not cut through the Sugar Dough. Push the end of a ball tool inside

this line three times, in the middle and to either side to make the hub caps. Set aside.

11 Using a flat, dry paintbrush, dust all the blue parts of Scrambler with Magic Sparkles to give a metallic effect.

12 To make the handlebars, you will need 3g (⅛oz) each of White and Black Sugar Dough. Roll each colour into a thin sausage shape and cut two 1.5cm (½") lengths in each colour and two small discs in black. Gently push a 5cm (2") length of 26-gauge white wire through the centre of a white and then a black sausage, and then into the top of the blue central part of the handlebars. Repeat on the other side, then attach a black disc at the end of each handle to cover the end of the wire.

13 Assemble all the pieces on top of the black base in the centre of the

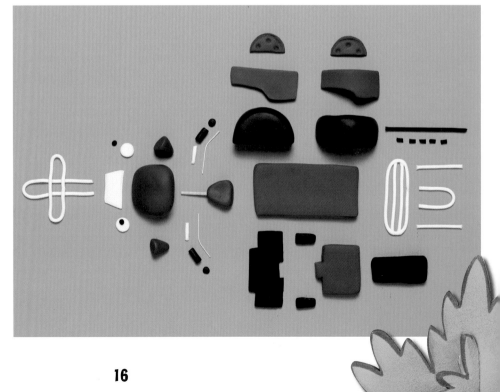

cake, securing in place with edible glue. When attaching the wheel arches, hold each one until firmly fixed or support with small pieces of food-grade foam sponge.

14 Cut 10g (¼oz) of Black Sugar Dough to shape for the footplate, as shown, and mark with the blunt edge of a knife. Secure between the arches and the blue base plate with edible glue. Knead and shape 10g (¼oz) of Black Sugar Dough into a seat approximately 1cm (¼") thick and mark with the knife as before. Secure to the back of Scrambler on the back plate.

15 Model 5g (just under ¼oz) of Black Sugar Dough into two side steps, mark as before and secure in place. Divide 200g (7oz) of Black Sugar Dough into four and shape two complete tyres. Cut each one in half, as if they are immersed in mud, and secure the hub caps in place. Secure the wheels to the top

of the cake under each wheel arch, positioning the two front wheels inward. For the tyre spikes, push 10g (¼oz) of softened Black Sugar Dough through a sugar shaper fitted with the round hole disc. Cut the extruded paste into very small pieces and attach to the tyres with edible glue.

16 Secure the back seat bar and back shelf section in place using edible glue, holding in place until firmly fixed. Secure the front grille in place.

17 Make the eyes from 5g (just under ¼oz) of White Sugar Dough and secure to the front of the blue cones. Add the pupils using the Black Sugar Dough trimmings.

18 Cut out a rectangle from White Sugar Dough for the mouth and press the grid embosser into the paste. Cut the corners at

an angle and then smooth around the edge with the blunt edge of the knife. Secure to the front of Scrambler.

19 Using a medium paintbrush, apply confectioners' glaze to all the blue pieces to seal in the dust and give the paste extra shine. Paint the white parts of the handlebars, the back grille and seat bar, the front grille section and mouth grille with edible silver paint.

Scruffty

20 Following the instructions on pages 20 to 21, make Scruffty and secure him to the seat of Scrambler.

Grass

21 Dust the dry grass sections with Daffodil Dust Food Colour in the centre and Shady Moss around the outer edges. You will need to colour one side of the larger pieces and both sides of the smaller ones. Draw a line along the inside edge of each piece using a Holly/Ivy Food Colour Pen.

22 Secure the larger sections of grass at six equal points around the base of the cake with edible glue and then secure the smaller sections to the centre of each one.

Mud

23 Melt the chocolate, following the instructions on the packet. Using a small spoon, spread the melted chocolate all around the base of Scrambler and around the wheels. Build up the chocolate a little at a time, adding more as it sets and letting some run down the sides of the cake. Add drops of chocolate to the wheel spikes, grilles, wheel arches and some on Scuffty. Drop small amounts of chocolate onto the cake drum, being careful not to add too much as it will merge into one big puddle!

To finish

24 Secure the ribbon to the edge of the cake drum using a non-toxic glue stick.

Important note: this cake contains inedible items such as wires and dowelling. Please ensure that these are safely removed before the cake is eaten.

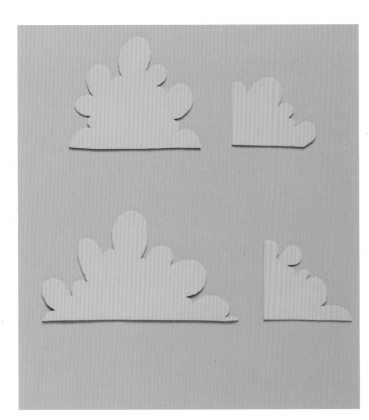

Scruffty in Mud

Materials

15cm (6") round sponge cake
225g (8oz) buttercream
SK Sugar Dough: 300g (10½oz) Green
100g (3½oz) SK Organic Milk Chocolate
Couverture

Equipment

20.5cm (8") round cake drum
65cm (26") x 1.5cm (½") width ribbon:
green
Non-toxic glue stick
Non-stick board and rolling pin
Closed curve crimpers (PME)
Small, sharp knife
Small spoon
Smoother

For the materials, equipment and
instructions required to make Scruffty, see
pages 20 to 21.

METHOD

Covering the cake

1 Cut and fill the sponge cake with
buttercream, then position the
cake centrally on the cake drum.
Cover the cake with a thin layer
of buttercream to help the Sugar
Dough stick to the cake.

2 Roll out the Green Sugar Dough
on a non-stick board dusted with
icing sugar and cover the cake.

Smooth down the top and sides with
a smoother and cut away any excess
paste at the base of the cake with a
small, sharp knife. Knead together the
Sugar Dough trimmings and roll out a
long strip. Cut a straight edge along
one side and cover the cake drum.
Smooth down any joins and trim the
excess paste from the edge using a
sharp knife. Crimp around the edge of
the cake drum for a neat finish.

Scruffty

3 Following the instructions on pages
20 to 21, make Scruffty and secure
him to the top of the cake.

4 Melt the chocolate, following the
instructions on the packet. Use a small
spoon to carefully drip small amounts
of chocolate around Scruffty's body,
covering the Green Sugar Dough. Build
up the mud puddle by adding more
melted chocolate on top, letting the
chocolate run down the sides of the
cake. Drip a little chocolate onto the top
of the head, paws, back of the body,
ears and around the base of the cake.

To finish

5 Secure the ribbon to the edge of the
cake drum using a non-toxic glue
stick.

SCRUFFTY

Materials

SK Sugar Dough: 3g (¹/₈oz) Black, 10g (¼oz) Brown, 150g (5¼oz) White

SK Paste Food Colours: Marigold, Poinsettia

SK Edible Paint: Gold

SK Edible Glue

White vegetable fat

Equipment

Dresden tool

Non-stick board

Paintbrush: medium

Small pieces of foam sponge or kitchen towel for support

METHOD

Body and legs

1 Reserve a small ball of White Sugar Dough to make the nose and collar disc later. Colour the remaining White Sugar Dough with Marigold Paste Food Colour.

2 Shape 60g (2oz) of the yellow paste into a pear shape for the body. Roll another 5g (just under ¼oz) into a long sausage shape approximately 1cm (¼") thick and cut it into four 2.5cm (1") lengths for the legs. Attach to the body with edible glue.

3 Divide 15g (½oz) of paste into four equal balls for the feet, model into shape and mark with the blunt side of a knife. Attach to the end of each leg.

4 Reserve a little Black Sugar Dough for the eyes. Knead the remaining paste into a disc and attach to the neck, between the front legs, to make the collar. Repeat the same process with a tiny amount of the reserved White Sugar Dough for the dog tag and attach to the side of the collar. Paint the tag with edible gold paint.

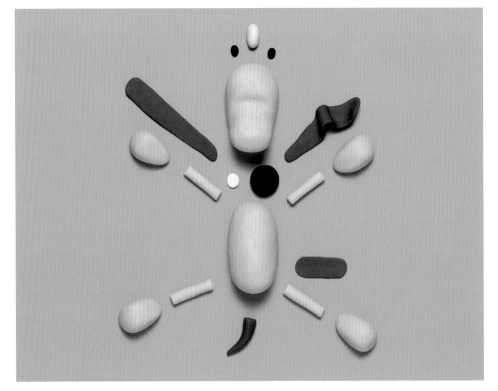

Collar

5 Mould the remaining 70g (2½oz) of Marigold-coloured Sugar Dough into another pear shape and bend slightly in the middle to form a muzzle at the fatter end. Mark the mouth with a Dresden tool and open it up slightly, then use the blunt edge of a knife to mark a central line at the top of the mouth. Secure the head to the collar with edible glue.

Mouth, patch and ears

6 Knead the Brown Sugar Dough and flatten a small piece to fit inside the mouth. Roll out some more Brown Sugar Dough and make a patch, then attach this to the middle of the body at the back. Divide the remaining Brown Sugar Dough to make a pair of ears, roll out two tapered strips approximately 6cm (2½") in length and round off the corners. Attach the narrow ends to

either side of the head and support with small pieces of foam sponge or rolled kitchen towel until dry.

Nose

7 Colour the remaining White Sugar Dough with a little Poinsettia Paste Food Colour to make a pale pink colour for the nose. Shape into an oval and secure to the head. Divide the reserved Black Sugar Dough in half for the eyes, roll each piece into a small ball, flatten between your fingers and secure to the head.

See how to make Scruffty's pawprint cupcakes on pages 58 to 61.

21

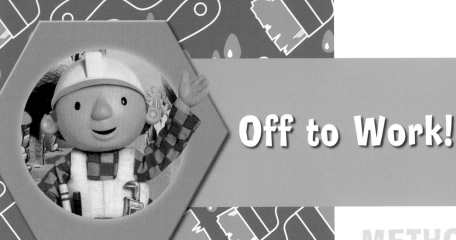

Off to Work!

Materials

2 x 20.5cm (8") round sponge cakes
625g (1lb 6oz) buttercream
SK Sugar Dough: 10g (¼oz) Black, pinch of Blue, 20g (¾oz) Brown, 5g (just under ¼oz) Golden Bear Brown, 700g (1lb 9oz) Green, 30g (1oz) Red, 175g (6oz) White, 5g (just under ¼oz) Yellow
SK Dust Food Colours: Daffodil, Shady Moss
SK Food Colour Pens: Blackberry, Holly/Ivy
SK Edible Paint: Silver
SK Edible Glue
Icing sugar in sugar shaker
Cooled, boiled water
Dried spaghetti
White vegetable fat

Equipment

30.5cm (12") round cake drum
127cm (50") x 1.5cm (½") width ribbon: green
Non-toxic glue stick
Non-stick board and rolling pin
Ball tool
Dresden tool
Paintbrushes: fine, medium
Small pieces food-grade foam sponge for support
Small, sharp knife
Smoother
Templates (see page 79)

For the materials, equipment and instructions required to make Bob, see pages 27 to 29.

METHOD
Covering the cake

1   Cut, fill and stack the sponge cakes. Take a sharp knife and carve the top of the cake into a dome shape. Position the cake towards the back of the cake drum and cover the whole cake with a thin layer of buttercream.

2   Roll out 500g (1lb 1¾oz) of Green Sugar Dough on a non-stick board and cover the cake. Smooth the surface with a smoother and cut away any excess paste at the base of the cake with a sharp knife. Reserve the trimmings for cake drum. Knead 150g (5¼oz) of White and 10g (¼oz) of Brown Sugar Dough together and roll out. Cut a length for the path down the front of the cake, tapering from 2.5cm (1") at the top to 16.5cm (6½") at the base of the cake. Secure the path to the front of the cake with edible glue and smooth over with a smoother.

Covering the cake drum

3 Knead together and roll out the brown trimmings into a strip to go at the front of the cake drum. Cut a straight edge using a sharp knife, dampen the cake drum with cooled, boiled water and fix in position. Roll out the reserved green trimmings into a strip, cut a straight edge, dampen the cake drum and secure in place. Cut to fit around the path at the front. Smooth over with a smoother and cut off any excess paste from around the edge of the cake drum.

Trees and grass

4 Roll out 200g (7oz) of Green Sugar Dough and cut six trees and six half-trees using the templates. Cut seven smaller trees with small mounds of grass and 12 sections of grass. Set aside to dry.

5 Dust the centre of the trees with Daffodil Dust Food Colour, then add Shady Moss around the edges (you only need to dust one side of the trees as the back won't be seen). Dust both sides of the half-trees with Shady Moss. Attach a half-tree section to the centre of the main tree using edible glue and secure to the cake drum. Position three trees on either side of the path.

6 Dust the grass sections with Daffodil and Shady Moss in the same way as for the trees, then draw an outline around each piece using a Holly/Ivy Food Colour Pen. Secure the grass to the side of the cake and on each side of the footpath around the base of the first tree using edible glue. If necessary,

you can position small amounts of Green Sugar Dough behind the shaped grass to help the grass stand up.

7 To make the small tree trunks, mix together small amounts of White and Brown Sugar Dough to make a light brown. Roll out the paste and cut seven tree trunks measuring 2.5cm (1") high and varying in width, depending on the size of

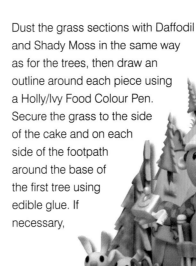

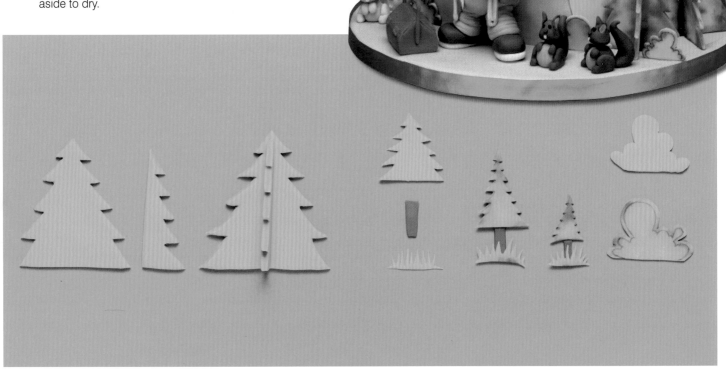

the treetops. Set aside. Dust the treetops and small grass mounds in the same way as before, then secure the tree trunks to the backs of the trees and grass mounds using edible glue. Attach to the cake with edible glue and add small amounts of Green Sugar Dough behind them for support.

Bunnies

8 Pinch two tiny balls of Blue Sugar Dough for the noses and reserve for later. Pinch two small balls of White Sugar Dough for the tails and two tiny amounts for teeth and set aside. Mix the rest of the Blue Sugar Dough with 10g (¼oz) of White Sugar Dough and divide into two.

9 Divide each of the balls of blue paste into pieces for the head, body, two ears, two front paws and two hind legs, following the step photograph as a guide. Mark

the features with a Dresden tool and push a small length of dried spaghetti into the neck. Assemble the body, limbs and tail using edible glue and push the head onto the body over the spaghetti.

10 Pinch two small balls of Black Sugar Dough for the eyes, flatten slightly and attach the eyes and nose to the face. Mark the underside of the nose and mouth opening with a small, sharp knife. Cut a small pair of teeth from White Sugar Dough and secure to the mouth opening with edible glue. Shape and bend the pair of ears and attach to the top of the head with edible glue, holding in place until secure.

Squirrels

11 Divide 10g (¼oz) of Brown Sugar Dough in half for the two squirrels. Divide each piece again into pieces

for the body, tail, two ears, two front paws, two hind legs and a head. Model each piece, following the step photograph as a guide. Divide the Golden Bear Brown Sugar Dough in half and model the inner ears and the front of the body for each squirrel. Mark the features with a Dresden tool and assemble the body, limbs and tail. Push a small length of dried spaghetti into the neck and secure the head in place.

12 Make two small eyes from Black Sugar Dough and a nose from Brown Sugar Dough and attach to the face using edible glue. Cut a small pair of teeth from a tiny amount of White Sugar Dough and secure beneath the nose.

Toolbox

13 To make the toolbox you will need 30g (1oz) of Red Sugar Dough. Roll out a small amount and cut four small rectangles for the hinges and mark with a small, sharp knife. Roll a thin sausage of paste measuring 9cm (3½") for the handle and set aside. Shape the remaining Red Sugar Dough into the toolbox shape and mark with the blunt edge of a small knife. Attach the hinges and the handle with edible glue.

Mallet

14 Divide 5g (just under ¼oz) of Black Sugar Dough in half. Roll one half into a sausage 4cm (1½") long and push a piece of dried spaghetti through the centre, leaving 0.5cm (¼")

exposed at the top. Roll the other half into a fat sausage 2cm (¾") long and secure to the spaghetti with edible glue. Set aside to dry.

Tape measure

15 Cut a strip from 3g (¹⁄₈oz) of White Sugar Dough and allow to dry slightly in a crumpled position. Pinch a small ball of White Sugar Dough for the handle, roll into a small sausage and bend at one end. Roll another small ball and attach to the bent end of the handle with edible glue. Shape the remaining White Sugar Dough into a 1cm (½") square 0.5cm (¼") thick and set aside. Add a small disc of Golden Bear Brown Sugar Dough to the top of the square and attach the handle to the top of the disc.

16 Mark the tape with a Blackberry Food Colour Pen and then attach this to one side of the white square. Paint the tape measure with edible silver paint.

Spirit level

17 Roll out 5g (just under ¼oz) of Yellow Sugar Dough to a thickness of 0.5cm (¼") and cut strip measuring 1.5cm x 6.5cm (½" x 2½"). Cut a small groove out of one side, then roll a small sausage of White Sugar Dough to fit inside the groove and secure with edible glue. Mark the centre with two lines and colour each end of the spirit level using a Blackberry Food Colour Pen. Set aside to dry.

Bob

18 Make Bob following the instructions on pages 27 to 29. Add the additional tools, tape measure in one hand and the mallet and spirit level under the other arm. Secure him to the front of the cake with edible glue.

To finish

19 Secure the toolbox to one side of Bob and position the bunnies to the side of it. Add the two squirrels on the other side of Bob and secure all the figures to the cake drum using edible glue.

20 Secure green ribbon to the edge of the cake drum with a non-toxic glue stick.

BOB

Materials

SK Sugar Dough: pinch of Black, 20g (¾oz) Blue, 20g (¾oz) Brown, 50g (1¾oz) Flesh, 80g (2¾oz) Orange, 100g (3½oz) White, 30g (1oz) Yellow
SK Paste Food Colour: Poinsettia
SK Edible Paint: Silver
SK Edible Glue
Cooled, boiled water or clear alcohol (e.g. gin or vodka)
Dried spaghetti
White vegetable fat

Equipment

Ball tool
Dresden tool
Paintbrushes: fine and medium
Small, sharp knife
10cm (4") length of thin dowelling (e.g. barbeque skewer)

METHOD

Tools

1. To make a screwdriver handle, take a small amount of Blue Sugar Dough and roll into a small, thin sausage shape. Break off a small length of dried spaghetti, approximately 2.5cm (1") long, dip the end into edible glue and the push into the end of the blue sausage shape. Round off the end and leave to dry. Repeat the same process with Yellow Sugar Dough. Model the wrench from a small amount of White Sugar Dough and mark with a Dresden tool. Leave to dry.

> **TIP**
>
> Allowing the head to dry upside down helps to keep chin rounded. The flat area at the top of the head will be covered by the hard hat.

Bob's head

2. Add a touch of Poinsettia Paste Food Colour to 50g (1¾oz) of Flesh Sugar Dough to make it a little pinker. Reserve three small balls for the ears and nose and two slightly larger balls for the hands. Roll the remaining paste into an oval shape for the head. Mark the mouth with a Dresden tool and gently mark under the bottom lip and the sides of the mouth up towards the nose area with the flat side of the same tool. Roll the nose into a pear shape and attach to the head with edible glue. Turn the head upside down and set aside to dry.

Boots

3 Add a pinch of Yellow Sugar Dough to 3g ($^1/_8$oz) of White Sugar Dough to make a cream colour. Divide in half and shape a sole for each boot. Reserve a small ball of Brown Sugar Dough for Bob's tool belt and another for the buckle, then roll two oval shapes from the remaining paste for the boots. Secure to the soles with edible glue.

Overalls

4 Reserve a small ball of White Sugar Dough to mix with the reserved brown paste. Mix together the rest of the White and the Blue Sugar Dough to make a lighter blue and knead well. Reserve a small ball for the straps and shape the rest into a fat sausage. Make a cut with a small, sharp knife to separate the legs, approximately 2.5cm (1") up from the base. Round off the cut area to shape the legs, then mark the overalls with a Dresden tool to create creases and a waistline for the belt.

5 Indent across the top of the shape with handle of the Dresden tool (this groove will eventually support the orange paste for the shirt), then flatten and square off the top edges with your finger and thumb. Roll out the small ball of blue paste reserved earlier and cut two straps measuring approximately 0.5cm (¼") wide and 2.5cm (1") long.

Shirt

6 Roll 80g (2¾oz) of Orange Sugar Dough into a sausage that is thicker in the middle and thinner at each end for the sleeves. Cut to size if necessary and attach inside the groove at the top of the overalls with edible glue. Mark creases in the sleeves with a Dresden tool and attach a strap over each shoulder, smoothing down any joins with your fingers. Push the end of the Dresden tool into the end of each sleeve to help secure the hands in place later.

7 Secure the body over the shoes with edible glue and push a small length of dowelling through the top of the shirt at the neck and into one leg and boot for more support.

Tool belt

8 Mix together the reserved White and Brown Sugar Dough, roll out and cut a strip to fit all the way around Bob's body, approximately 0.5cm (¼") wide. Cut four shorter pieces the

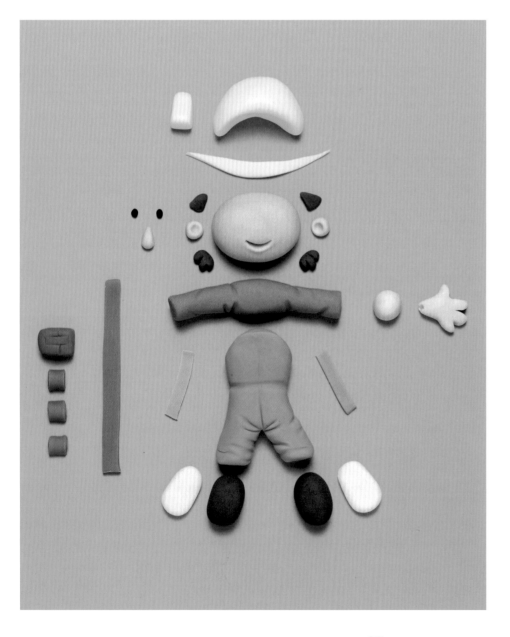

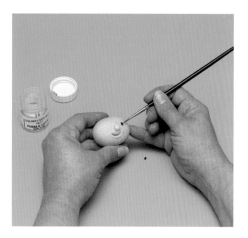

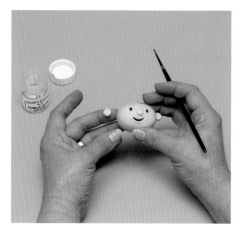

same width, three to hold the tools and another to fit inside the buckle. Shape the remaining Sugar Dough into a square shape for the pouch and mark the opening with the tip of a small knife.

9 Using a fine paintbrush, paint the dried spaghetti parts on the prepared tools and the wrench with edible silver paint. Attach each tool to the belt with edible glue and then curve the short belt pieces over the top and secure in place. Add the pouch at the side of the wrench. Roll out the remaining light brown Sugar Dough and cut a square for the buckle, attach to the last section of the belt and secure both to the belt with edible glue.

Hands

10 Take the two larger balls of Flesh Sugar Dough reserved earlier and shape into hands. Use a small, sharp knife to cut three fingers and a thumb. Soften the cut edges with your fingers to round off the fingers and thumb.

11 Mould the end of each hand to a small point, brush a little SK Edible sugar glue into the end of each of

the shirt sleeves and push each hand up inside. Hold in place until they are secured into position.

Chequered shirt

12 Paint the squares on Bob's shirt with Poinsettia Paste Food Colour diluted with a little cooled, boiled water or clear alcohol. Allow to dry.

Bob's face

13 Turn the head the right way up and push a little Black Sugar Dough into the mouth opening with the end of a Dresden tool. Gently push the head over the dowelling rod and secure at the neck with a little edible glue. Use the two remaining small balls of Flesh Sugar Dough to make the ears and push the end of a ball tool into each one. Attach to the side of the head.

14 Use the remaining Brown Sugar Dough for the hair. Roll two small balls for the hair at the top of the ears, shape and attach in place. Shape the remaining paste into a sausage shape, mark hair lines with a Dresden tool and attach to the back of the head with edible glue.

15 Make two tiny ovals for the eyes from Black Sugar Dough and attach either side of the nose.

Hard hat

16 Knead 30g (1oz) of Yellow Sugar Dough, reserve 5g (just under ¼oz) for the front section and the peak, and shape the rest into a dome shape, making sure it fits on top of the head snugly. Secure into position with edible glue.

17 Shape the front section into a triangular shape, cut to size with a small, sharp knife and attach to the front. To make the peak, roll out the remaining yellow paste into a thin strip and cut a straight edge on one side and a curved shape on the other. Cut to size and attach at the base of the helmet with edible glue.

Bob's Toolbox

Materials

20.5cm (8") square sponge cake
450g (1lb) buttercream
SK Sugar Dough: 10g (¼oz) Black, 10g (¼oz) Blue, 25g (just over ¾oz) Brown, 420g (14¾oz) Green, 650g (1lb 7oz) Red, 200g (7oz) White, 20g (¾oz) Yellow
SK Edible Paint: Gold, Silver
SK Edible Glue
Icing sugar in sugar shaker
Cooled, boiled water or clear alcohol
Dried spaghetti
White vegetable fat

Equipment

30.5cm (12") square cake drum
127cm (50") x 1.5cm (½") width ribbon: green
Non-toxic glue stick
Non-stick board and rolling pin
1 x 20-gauge floristry wire: white
Ball tool
Dresden tool
Paintbrush: medium
Rectangle and circle cutters (CT)
Small pieces food-grade foam sponge or kitchen towel for support
Small, sharp knife
Smoother
Template (see page 79)

For the materials, equipment and instructions required to make Bird, see pages 34 to 35.

METHOD
Covering the cake drum

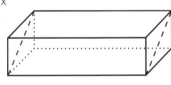

1 Roll out 400g (14oz) of Green Sugar Dough on a non-stick board, dampen the cake drum with cooled, boiled water and cover the cake drum with the Sugar Dough. Smooth over the surface of the paste with a smoother and trim the excess paste from around the edge with a small, sharp knife. Set aside to dry.

Toolbox

2 Cut the crusts off the cake, keeping the cake square. Cut an 8cm (3") wide piece from one side of the cake to leave a 20.5cm x 13cm (8" x 5") rectangle. Trim a further 1.5cm (½") from the long side of the smaller piece to give a 6cm x 20.5cm (2½" x 8") rectangle, then cut this piece diagonally, starting at the long side and cutting from corner to corner through the ends to give two triangular shapes. Turn the pieces so that they are back to back to create the top section of the toolbox (the two shortest sides of the triangle should fit the top of the rectangle). Fill the cake with buttercream, attach the top triangular section and spread a layer of buttercream over the surface of the cake.

3 Knead and roll out 600g (1lb 5¼oz) of Red Sugar Dough on a non-stick board and cover the whole cake. Smooth down the top and sides with a smoother and cut away any excess paste at the base of the cake with a small, sharp knife. Position the cake on the prepared cake drum at an angle,

towards the back of the board. Mark the opening of the toolbox at the top, sides, front and back with the blunt side of a small, sharp knife.

4 Roll out 40g (1½oz) of Red Sugar Dough and cut eight rectangles with the cutter set. Take a smaller cutter and cut away two rectangles on one side, one on the edge and the other in the middle. Make sure that you cut four alternatives so the hinges will slot together when attached to the side of the toolbox. Secure to the side/top of the toolbox with edible glue. Knead the trimmings together and roll again, then cut 16 small discs with the circle cutters and attach one in each corner of each hinge.

5 Roll the remaining Red Sugar Dough into a long sausage shape approximately 38cm (15") in length. Cut a straight edge at each end with a sharp knife and bend the handle into shape. Rest the handle at the back of the tool box, attach each

end to the middle of the tool box with edible glue and support with small pieces of foam sponge or rolled kitchen towel until dry.

Blue screwdriver

6 Roll 10g (¼oz) of Blue Sugar Dough into a sausage shape. Roll a thinner length from 5g (just under ¼oz) of White Sugar Dough, flatten one end and shape. Push a 5cm (2") length of dried spaghetti into the centre, leaving half exposed. Brush a little edible glue on one end of the blue handle and push the exposed spaghetti into the handle. Set aside to dry.

Yellow screwdriver

7 Roll 20g (¾oz) of Yellow Sugar Dough into a sausage shape as before, flatten both ends and mark one end with the blunt edge of a

knife. Push a 5cm (2") length of dried spaghetti into the centre, leaving half exposed. Cut the other end into two sections for the red to be inserted. Make two discs from Red Sugar Dough to the same width as the handle and secure the red and yellow pieces in place with edible glue. Make the screwdriver end in the same way as before and secure to the handle. Set aside to dry.

Hammer

8 Roll 25g (just over ¾oz) of Brown Sugar Dough into a handle shape and push a 5cm (2") length of dried spaghetti into the centre, leaving a third exposed. Shape 5g (just under ¼oz) of White Sugar Dough into the hammer head pieces, as shown. Assemble the hammer head together with edible glue, then brush a little glue around the handle top and push the exposed spaghetti into the hammer. Set aside to dry.

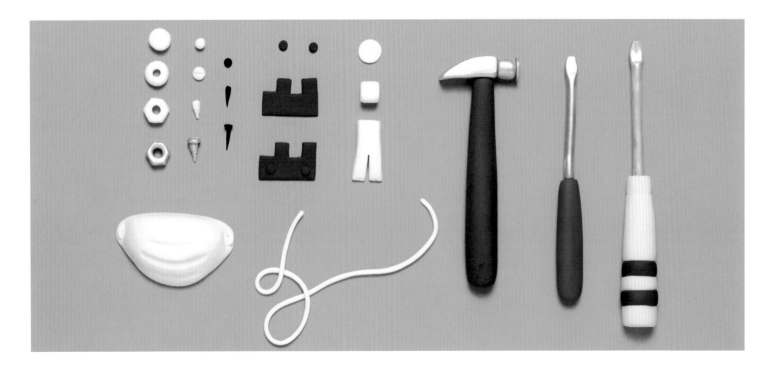

Spanner

9 Roll out 20g (¾oz) of White Sugar Dough to a thickness of 1cm (¼") and cut out the shape of a spanner from the template. Run a ball tool across the centre of the handle to form an indentation. Set aside to dry.

Mask

10 Shape 50g (1¾oz) of White Sugar Dough into an oval dome shape and place pieces of foam sponge underneath to give support whilst drying. Slightly flatten either side of the mask and push a Dresden tool into the surface twice to attach the ties. Mark three indentations across the front with a ball tool. Roll long, thin pieces for the ties and secure in place with edible glue. Set aside to dry.

Trowel

11 Roll out 50g (1¾oz) of White Sugar Dough and cut a diamond shape that is longer at one end. Roll the trimmings into a sausage shape measuring 8cm (3") long. Flatten one end and attach to the diamond shape with edible glue, smoothing down any joins. Push a 15cm (6") length of wire into the top of the sausage and through to the bottom of the trowel. Bend the wire downwards to support the handle. Roll 10g (¼oz) of Green Sugar Dough into a sausage, round off one end and cut a straight edge at the other end. Brush a little edible glue on the cut edge and insert the wire into the centre of the handle. Set aside to dry, supporting the handle if necessary with pieces of foam sponge or rolled kitchen towel.

Nuts

12 Divide 10g (¼oz) of White Sugar Dough into several equally sized balls and flatten to a thickness of 1cm (¼"). Push the end of a Dresden tool into the centre to form a hole and push through the other side to neaten the edge. Whilst the Sugar Dough is on the Dresden tool, pinch the sides between your finger and thumb to create six flat sides. Set aside to dry.

Screws

13 Roll 5g (just under ¼oz) of White Sugar Dough into a number of small balls and flatten slightly between your finger and thumb. Mark across the top of each one with the blunt edge of a small knife. Roll the trimmings together and make the ends for the screws by rolling small cone shapes. Mark each one diagonally with the blunt side of a small knife and secure to the heads of the screws with edible glue. Set aside to dry.

Tacks

14 Thinly roll out 10g (¼oz) of Black Sugar Dough and cut out several small circles using the smallest cutter from the set. Roll up the trimmings and make the pointed ends of the tacks. Attach to the discs with edible glue.

Bird

15 If required, you can place Bird beside the toolbox to add character to the cake! Full instructions for making Bird can be found on pages 34 to 35.

To finish

16 Paint the tools, nuts and screws with edible silver or gold paint and secure into position over the covered cake drum with edible glue.

17 Secure green ribbon around the edge of the cake drum using a non-toxic glue stick.

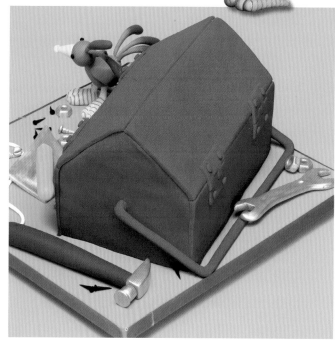

BIRD

Materials

SK Sugar Dough: pinch of Black, 25g (just over ¾oz) Blue, 25g (just over ¾oz) White, 15g (½oz) Yellow
SK Food Colour Pen: Poinsettia
SK Dust Food Colours: Daffodil and Poinsettia
SK Edible Glue
White vegetable fat

Equipment

1 x 26-gauge floristry wire: white
Dresden tool
Paintbrushes: medium, flat
Scissors
Small, sharp knife

METHOD

Feet

1 Knead two 5g (just under ¼oz) portions of Yellow Sugar Dough for the feet. Mould into shape, as shown, and mark the toes halfway up each foot with the blunt edge of a small knife. Cut two pieces of white wire, each measuring 4cm (1½") long, and push into the top part of the leg and down into the foot, leaving approximately 1.5cm (½") exposed at the top. Set aside to dry.

Body, head and wings

2 Mix the Blue and White Sugar Dough together to make a lighter blue colour and divide up into seven 5g (just under ¼oz) portions as follows: one for the head, one for each of the five feathers (three for the tail and two for the head), and divide one in half for the wings. Use the remaining paste for the body.

3 For each of the feathers, roll the paste into a sausage, making it thinner at one end. Cut a length of wire approximately 5cm (2") long for each feather, insert it into the thin end of the paste, leaving approximately 1.5cm (½") exposed at the end, and curve it slightly. Set aside to dry.

4 Make two flattened triangles for the wings, round off the corners and mark along one side with the blunt edge of a small knife.

5 Roll the last portion of paste into a ball for the head and set aside.

6 Shape the remaining blue paste into a curved shape for the body, as

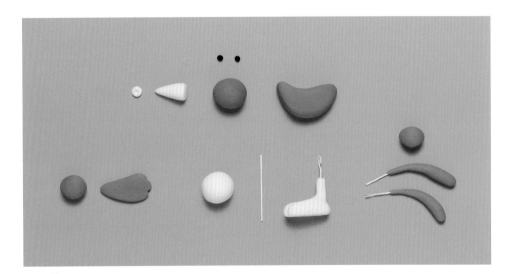

34

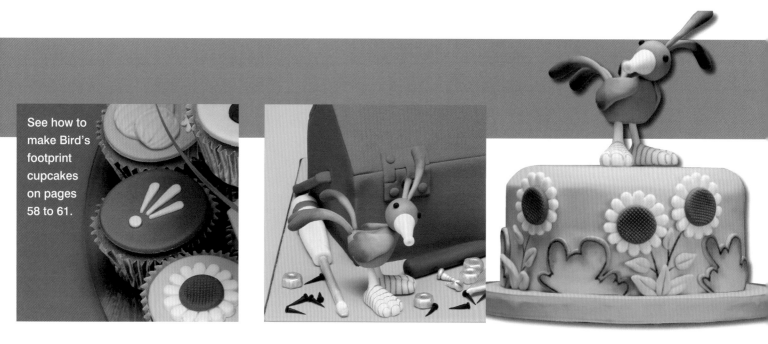

See how to make Bird's footprint cupcakes on pages 58 to 61.

shown. Cut a 2.5cm (1") length of wire and insert it into the neck, leaving some protruding from the top. Set aside.

7 Knead 3g (⅛") of Yellow Sugar Dough and take off a small ball for the end of the beak. Shape the rest into a long cone and attach the small ball to the pointed end, securing in place with edible glue. Push the end of a Dresden tool into the centre of the ball to mark the indent.

8 Using a dry, flat paintbrush, dust the wings and the feathers with Poinsettia Dust Food Colour. Next, mix some Poinsettia and Daffodil Dusts together to make a lighter colour and brush this onto the tips.

Assembly

9 To assemble Bird, push the wired feet into the underside of the body and secure in place with edible glue. Allow to dry completely before

attaching the wings to either side of the body, holding them in place until they are securely fixed. Push three feathers into the bottom end of the body and secure with edible glue. Fix the head in the same way, then push the last two feathers into the top of the head and secure. Fix the beak to the front of the head, holding it in place until firmly attached. Lastly, divide the pinch of Black Sugar Dough in half, roll two small balls for the eyes and attach to the head.

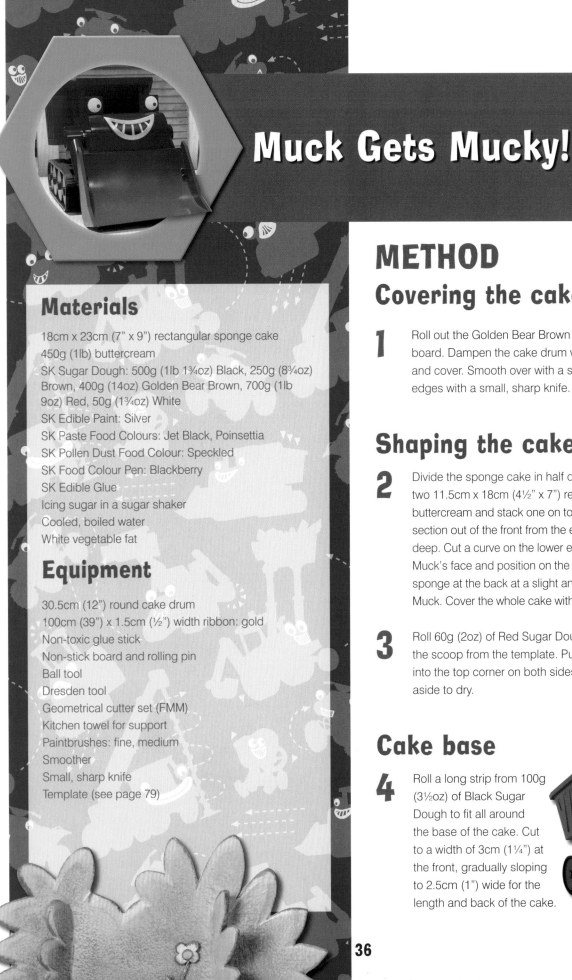

Muck Gets Mucky!

METHOD
Covering the cake drum

1 Roll out the Golden Bear Brown Sugar Dough on a non-stick board. Dampen the cake drum with cooled, boiled water and cover. Smooth over with a smoother and trim around the edges with a small, sharp knife. Set aside.

Materials

18cm x 23cm (7" x 9") rectangular sponge cake
450g (1lb) buttercream
SK Sugar Dough: 500g (1lb 1¾oz) Black, 250g (8¾oz) Brown, 400g (14oz) Golden Bear Brown, 700g (1lb 9oz) Red, 50g (1¾oz) White
SK Edible Paint: Silver
SK Paste Food Colours: Jet Black, Poinsettia
SK Pollen Dust Food Colour: Speckled
SK Food Colour Pen: Blackberry
SK Edible Glue
Icing sugar in a sugar shaker
Cooled, boiled water
White vegetable fat

Equipment

30.5cm (12") round cake drum
100cm (39") x 1.5cm (½") width ribbon: gold
Non-toxic glue stick
Non-stick board and rolling pin
Ball tool
Dresden tool
Geometrical cutter set (FMM)
Kitchen towel for support
Paintbrushes: fine, medium
Smoother
Small, sharp knife
Template (see page 79)

Shaping the cake

2 Divide the sponge cake in half down the long side to make two 11.5cm x 18cm (4½" x 7") rectangles. Fill both halves with buttercream and stack one on top of the other. Cut a 2.5cm (1") section out of the front from the edge, measuring 4cm (1½") deep. Cut a curve on the lower edge of cake for the front of Muck's face and position on the prepared cake drum. Cut the sponge at the back at a slight angle to shape the tipper body of Muck. Cover the whole cake with a thin layer of buttercream.

3 Roll 60g (2oz) of Red Sugar Dough and cut the two sides of the scoop from the template. Push the end of a paintbrush into the top corner on both sides of the Sugar Dough. Set aside to dry.

Cake base

4 Roll a long strip from 100g (3½oz) of Black Sugar Dough to fit all around the base of the cake. Cut to a width of 3cm (1¼") at the front, gradually sloping to 2.5cm (1") wide for the length and back of the cake.

5 Roll out 100g (3½oz) of Red Sugar Dough and cut three strips, each measuring 2.5cm x 11.5cm (1" x 4½"). Attach one to the back of the cake above the Black Sugar Dough and one either side of the cake. Smooth over the surface with a smoother to disguise any joins.

Panels

6 Roll another 100g (3½oz) of Red Sugar Dough and cut two sections measuring 7cm x 6cm (2¾" x 2½"). Shape the curved front ends of both pieces to match the front of the cake, attach to the sides and neaten with a smoother.

7 To make the front panel, roll out 100g (3½oz) of Red Sugar Dough and cut a panel measuring 9.5cm x 8cm (4¾" x 3¼"). Secure to the front of the cake above the Black Sugar Dough and smooth over using a smoother.

Front scoop

8 Roll out 100g (3½oz) of Red Sugar Dough and cut a 13cm x 10cm (5" x 4") panel. Attach to the front of the cake on the front panel, curve round and rest the base on the cake drum. Secure in place with edible glue. Lift up the front edge of the scoop very slightly and support with folded kitchen towel. Attach the side pieces made earlier to either side of the scoop using edible glue.

Cab

9 Roll out 30g (1oz) of White Sugar Dough and cut a rectangle measuring 19cm x 4cm (7½" x 1½"). Attach to the cake above the front panel and sides. Smooth down with a smoother. Model six pillars from Red Sugar Dough measuring 0.5cm x 4cm (¼" x 1½") and attach to the front and sides of the cab with edible glue. Roll out 60g (2oz) of Red Sugar Dough to

a thickness of 0.5cm (¼"), cut a 13cm x 4.5cm (5" x 1¾") rectangle for the roof of the cab and secure on the top of the White Sugar Dough. Smooth over with a smoother.

Black panel

10 Roll out 100g (3½oz) of Black Sugar Dough and cut a strip measuring 2cm x 28cm (¾" x 11"). Attach to the cake behind the red side panels, over the top of the cake and down to the other side. Cut another length to go around the back of the cake measuring 1.5cm x 29cm (½" x 11½") and attach above the Red Sugar Dough. Cut to fit and smooth down.

Tipper body

11 Roll out 250g (8¾oz) of Red Sugar Dough to a 0.5cm (¼") thickness. Cut a back panel measuring 13cm x 7cm (5" x 2¾") and two side panels measuring (4") across the top, 9cm (3½") across the base, 7cm (2¾") up one side, then cut a diagonal line up the fourth side. Attach all three pieces to the cake and smooth. Using a ball tool, mark three vertical lines down the Sugar Dough and make a small mark in the corner of both side panels.

12 Knead together the trimmings and roll a strip 0.5cm (¼") thick. Cut two lengths measuring 15cm x 1.5cm (5" x ½") and two lengths measuring 11cm x 1.5cm (4¼" x ½"). Attach the two longer lengths to the top of the side panels and the shorter lengths to the back and front of the tipper, resting on the roof of the cab.

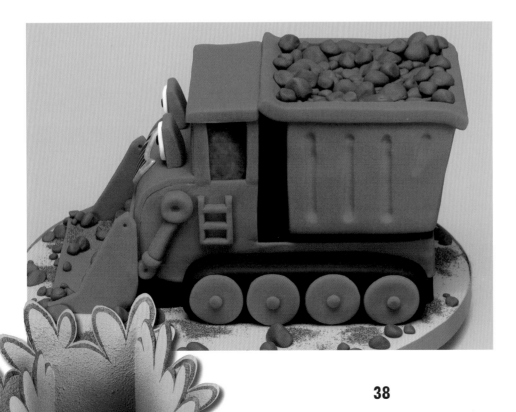

Rocks

13 Model several rock shapes from 200g (7oz) of Brown Sugar Dough and push into the top of the cake. Build up the rocks until the tipper is full. Reserve some Brown Sugar Dough to make more rocks later.

Side wheels

14 Divide 300g (10½oz) of Black Sugar Dough in half and roll two fat sausage shapes with rounded ends. Flatten to a thickness of 2cm (¾") and attach one to each side of Muck. Roll out 40g (1½oz) of Red Sugar Dough, cut eight circles from the geometrical cutter set and secure four to each side with edible glue. Knead the trimmings together and roll eight small balls to fit in the middle of each wheel. Secure in place.

Side ladders

15 Roll out a small ball of Red Sugar Dough and cut two ladders, following the template. Secure one on each side of Muck with edible glue.

Side arms

16 Divide 20g (¾oz) of Red Sugar Dough into two medium balls, flatten slightly for the top of the arms and attach to the side of the cake with edible glue. Push the end of a ball tool into the centre of each one. Roll two lengths measuring 2.5cm (1") long and 1cm (³/₈") thick and attach under the previous circles at an angle on both sides. Roll four balls and flatten slightly to measure approximately 1.5cm (½") wide. Attach two on either side, one behind

the scoop and the other on its side between the length and disc. Push the end of a paintbrush into the bottom disc behind the scoop on both sides.

17 Dilute some Poinsettia Paste Food Colour with a little cooled, boiled water or clear alcohol and paint the inside of the cab and the White Sugar Dough. Dilute some Jet Black Paste Food Colour and paint the top corners and front of the cab to create shading.

Eyes

18 Roll out 10g (¼oz) of Red Sugar Dough to a 0.5cm (¼") thickness and cut two 2.5cm (1") squares. Roll out some White Sugar Dough, cut two circles to fit inside the squares and attach with edible glue. Pinch two small balls of Black Sugar Dough, flatten and attach to the eyes. Secure the whole sections onto the top of the front panel.

Mouth

19 Roll out 10g (¼oz) of White Sugar Dough and cut a mouth using the template. Draw the teeth with a Blackberry Food Colour Pen and paint the outline of the mouth with edible silver paint. Allow to dry and then attach to the front with edible glue.

To finish

20 Make more rocks from the remaining Brown Sugar Dough and attach them to the cake drum and inside the tipper with edible glue. Brush areas on the cake drum and scoop with edible glue and sprinkle small amounts of Speckled Pollen Dust Food Colour over the glue.

21 Attach gold ribbon to the edge of the cake drum using a non-toxic glue stick.

Building in Progress

Materials

20.5cm (8") square sponge cake
450g (1lb) buttercream
SK Sugar Dough: 10g (¼oz) Black, 50g (1¾oz) Blue,
25g (just over ¾oz) Brown, 600g (1lb 5½oz) Flesh,
250g (8¾oz) Golden Bear Brown, pinch of Green, 80g
(2¾oz) Orange, 30g (1oz) Red, 110g (3¾oz) White,
30g (1oz) Yellow
SK Paste Food Colours: Bulrush, Chestnut, Poinsettia
SK Food Colour Pen: Blackberry
SK Edible Paint: Silver
SK Edible Glue
SK Edible Photograph
Icing sugar in sugar shaker
Cooled, boiled water or clear alcohol
Dried spaghetti
White vegetable fat

Equipment

30.5cm (12") square cake drum
127cm (50") x 1.5cm (½") width ribbon: gold
Non-toxic glue stick
Non-stick board and rolling pin
1 x 26-gauge floristry wire: white
Ball tool
Dresden tool
Impression mats: tree bark and brick wall (FMM set 1)
Paintbrush: medium
Rectangle cutters (CT)
Small, sharp knife
Smoother

**For the materials, equipment and instructions
required to make Bob, see pages 27 to 29;
for Pilchard, see page 44.**

METHOD
Covering the cake

1 Cut and fill the cake with buttercream, then position the cake towards the back of the cake drum. Cover the cake with a thin layer of buttercream.

2 Roll out 200g (7oz) of Flesh Sugar Dough on a non-stick board and cut a 20.5cm (8") square. Place the square on top of the cake and smooth over the surface with a smoother. Bring the corners and edges down the sides of the cake slightly.

3 Roll out 300g (10½oz) of Flesh Sugar Dough to a thickness of 0.5cm (¼"). Cut four pieces to fit the sides of the cake, measuring approximately 22cm x 7cm (8½" x 2¾"), and secure to the sides of the cake. Press the brick wall impression mat into the four sides of the cake.

4 Knead the trimmings together, roll out again and push the impression mat into the Sugar Dough. Take a small, sharp knife and cut around the brick shapes to give a staggered effect to the brickwork, not going any higher than four bricks. Cut a straight edge to go into the corner, then turn the brickwork over and press the mat into the Sugar Dough to mark the back of the bricks. Attach the bricks to the top of the brickwork around the cake towards the two back corners. Secure with edible glue.

Bricks

5 Roll out 100g (3½oz) of Flesh Sugar Dough to a thickness of 0.5cm (¼"). Using a rectangle cutter, cut out approximately 35 individual bricks and set aside to dry.

6 To paint the bricks, dilute a little Poinsettia Paste Food Colour with cooled, boiled water to make a pale pink colour wash and paint random bricks on the sides of the cake and a selection of loose bricks. Repeat the same process with Bulrush and Chestnut Paste Food Colours respectively. Leave some of the loose bricks unpainted.

Covering the cake drum

7 Roll out 250g (8¾oz) of Golden Bear Brown Sugar Dough on a non-stick board. Roll a strip long enough to fit around the base of the cake and cut a straight edge along one side. Dampen the surface of the cake drum with cooled, boiled water and secure the paste to the drum. Cut to size, smooth over the surface and finish with a smoother. Run a sharp knife around the edge of the cake drum to cut away excess paste.

Board and cement

8 Roll out 10g (¼oz) of Brown Sugar Dough and cut out a 5cm (2") square. Attach this to the front of the cake at an angle with edible glue. Build up the cement roughly using Flesh Sugar Dough, mark with a Dresden tool and attach to the board with edible glue.

9 For the handle of the trowel, mix a small amount of White Sugar Dough with a tiny pinch of Black Sugar Dough to make a light grey. Roll into a thin sausage shape and push a 4cm (1½") length of 26-gauge white wire into the paste, leaving the wire exposed on both sides of the paste. Bend each end at a 90° angle to create a 'Z' shape. Roll a thin sausage of Green Sugar Dough and cut to size to match the grey piece. Secure over one end of the wire for the handle. Push the exposed wire into the cement on the board, securing in place with a little edible glue.

Mallet

10 Make the mallet from 5g (just under ¼oz) of Black Sugar Dough, following the instructions given on the Off to Work! cake on page 26. Allow to dry.

Wheelbarrow

11 To make the wheel, roll 5g (just under ¼oz) of Blue Sugar Dough into a ball, flatten the wheel and set aside to dry. Mix together 15g (½oz) of Blue and 10g of White Sugar Dough to make a light blue. Roll out and cut into five rectangles: 6cm x

4cm (2¼" x 1½") for the base, 4cm x 2.5cm (1½" x 1") for the front panel, 4cm x 0.5cm (1½" x ½") for the back panel, and two 4.5cm x 2.5cm (1¾" x 1") side panels. Set aside to dry. Model the handles and barrow rests from 10g (¼oz) of Brown Sugar Dough and set aside to dry.

12 To assemble the wheelbarrow secure the side, top and back panels to the base with edible glue and hold in place until secure. Attach the brown handles and rests to the underside of the wheelbarrow, leaving enough room for the wheel to fit between them at the front. When dry, secure the wheel in place and hold until firmly fixed.

Tape measure

13 Make the tape measure following the instructions given on the Off to Work! cake on page 26. Allow to dry.

Toolbox

14 Make the toolbox from 30g (1oz) of Red Sugar Dough, following the instructions given on the Off to Work! cake on page 26. Allow to dry.

Pilchard

15 Make Pilchard following the instructions on page 44. Support the tail against the side of the cake with two prepared bricks attached to the top of the cake, as if they are to about to tumble.

Bob

16 Make Bob following the instructions on pages 27 to 29. Secure him to the cake board at the front of the cake, using the side of the cake as support.

Edible photograph

17 Roll out 100g (3½oz) of White Sugar Dough and cut a rectangle measuring 18cm x 10.5cm (7" x 4¼") to fit underneath the photograph of your choice. Follow the instructions supplied with the photograph and secure to the top of the prepared white rectangle. Secure the mounted photo to the top of the cake with edible glue.

To finish

18 Attach the mallet underneath the wheelbarrow and secure some loose bricks inside the wheelbarrow with edible glue. Secure more loose bricks to the top of the cake and the cake drum.

19 Attach gold ribbon to the sides of the cake drum with a non-toxic glue stick.

TIP
You can use an edible photograph of the recipient for the cake top, or write a special inscription in Sugar Dough using an alphabet cutter set.

43

PILCHARD

Materials

SK Sugar Dough: 5g (just under ¼oz)
Black, 20g (¾oz) Blue, 10g (¼oz)
White
SK Food Colour Pen: Blackberry
SK Edible Glue
White vegetable fat

Equipment

1 x 26-gauge floristry
wire: white
Paintbrush: medium
Scissors
Small, sharp knife
Tweezers

METHOD

Head, body, feet and tail

1   Mix together the Blue and White Sugar Dough to create a lighter blue. Knead the Black Sugar Dough. Divide both colours into sections for the head and ears, body, feet and tail and model into the required shapes, following the photograph as a guide.

2   Cut four lengths of white wire, approximately 2cm (¾") long, and colour each one with a Blackberry Food Colour Pen for the whiskers. Set aside.

3   Assemble the pieces for the tail, brushing a little edible glue between each of the colours to secure them in place. Mould into the required position and set aside to dry completely.

4   Attach the nose at the front of the head, then mark the mouth with the food pen, starting from the underside of the nose. Add the eyes and ears and then the whiskers, using tweezers to push them into the head.

Assembly

5   To assemble Pilchard, mark the two front feet with the blunt edge of a small knife and position them at the front of the body. Secure three black stripes over the body with edible glue. Mark the two back feet in the same way, position at the back of the body, then secure in place.

6   Secure the head to the front of the body, over the front paws, with edible glue.

7   Attach the dry tail to the back end of Pilchard and support with pieces of foam or Sugar Dough until it is firmly fixed in position.

TIP

If Pilchard is lying down, you do not need to make his feet. Instead, wrap his tail around the base of the body. This saves time as the tail does not need to dry firm.

Hello, Bob!

Materials

15cm (6") round sponge cake
225g (8oz) buttercream
SK Sugar Dough: 5g (just under ¼oz) Black, 200g (7oz) Blue, 10g (¼oz) Brown, 250g (8¾oz) Flesh, pinch of White, 250g (8¾oz) Yellow
SK Paste Food Colour: Poinsettia
SK Edible Glue
Icing sugar in sugar shaker
Cooled, boiled water or clear alcohol
White vegetable fat

Equipment

25.5cm (10") round cake drum
86cm (34") x 1.5cm (½") width ribbon: blue
Non- toxic glue stick
Non-stick board and large and small rolling pins
Dresden tool
Small, sharp knife
Smoother

METHOD
Covering the cake

1 Fill the centre of the sponge cake with buttercream and position centrally on the cake drum. Trim the top of the cake with a sharp knife to make it more rounded and cover with a layer of buttercream.

2 Add a touch of Poinsettia Paste Food Colour to the Flesh Sugar Dough to make a pinker colour for Bob's face. Reserve 25g (just over ¾oz) of the Flesh Sugar Dough for the ears and nose, then roll out the remaining paste on a non-stick board dusted with icing sugar. Cut a straight edge for the top of the face and cover the lower two thirds of the cake. Smooth over the top and sides with a smoother, trim away any excess paste at the base of the cake and smooth down the cut edge.

3 Make a shallow mouth opening with a Dresden tool, attach a thin, rolled length of Flesh Sugar Dough for the bottom lip and smooth down any joins. Fill the inside of the mouth with a thin piece of Black Sugar Dough and push the paste into the corners of the mouth with the Dresden tool.

4 Reserve 50g (1¾oz) of Yellow Sugar Dough for the peak and trim of the hard hat for later. Roll out the remaining Yellow Sugar Dough, cut a straight edge to match up with the top of Bob's face and cover the top part of the cake. Smooth over the top and sides with a smoother, trim away any excess paste from the base of the cake and smooth over the cut areas.

Covering the cake drum

5 Roll out the Blue Sugar Dough to form a long strip that will fit all the way around Bob's head. Cut a straight edge along one side, dampen the cake drum with a little cooled, boiled water and attach the blue strip with the straight edge at the base of the covered cake. Cut to size and smooth over any joins with a smoother. Trim away any excess paste from the edge of the cake drum with a small, sharp knife.

Ears

6 Roll 10g (¼oz) of Flesh Sugar Dough into a ball for each ear, and then push the end of a small rolling pin into the centre to mark each ear. Attach to the side of the head on the covered cake drum with edible glue.

Hair

7 Divide 10g (¼oz) of Brown Sugar Dough into four balls for the hair above and below the ears. Shape and mark each piece with a Dresden tool and attach into position with edible glue.

Nose

8 Shape the remaining 5g (just under ¼oz) of Flesh Sugar Dough into a pear shape, slightly flatten the base and attach to the front of the face between the mouth and the hard hat with edible glue.

Eyes

9 Divide the Black Sugar Dough in half for the eyes, shape into rounded ovals and attach to the face with edible glue, level with the top of the nose. Put tiny highlights in the eyes by adding a piece of White Sugar Dough at the top of each one.

Hard hat

10 To make the front piece for the hard hat, shape 25g (just over ¾oz) of Yellow Sugar Dough into a squared-off triangle and attach this to the hard hat with the thicker part at the top and thinner end at the base of the hat.

11 Roll the remaining 25g (just over ¾oz) of Yellow Sugar Dough into a strip, cut a straight edge on one side and a curve on the other. The widest part at the centre should measure approximately 2.5cm (1") wide and the ends should taper to a point. Cut to size to fit the base of the hat and secure in place with edible glue.

To finish

12 Attach blue ribbon to the edge of the cake drum using a non-toxic glue stick.

Stinky Spud and Wild Patch Go West!

Materials

20.5cm (8") square sponge cake
450g (1lb) buttercream
SK Sugar Dough: 100g (3½oz) Black, 100g (3½oz) Blue, 30g (1oz) Brown, 700g (1lb 9oz) Flesh, 100g (3½oz) Golden Bear Brown, 250g (8¾oz) Green, 50g (1¾oz) Maroon, 250g (8¾oz) Orange, 5g (just under ¼oz) Red, 400g (14oz) White
SK Paste Food Colours: Berberis, Chestnut, Poinsettia
SK Clear Piping Gel
SK Edible Glue
Icing sugar in a sugar shaker
Cooled, boiled water or clear alcohol
White vegetable fat

Equipment

30.5cm (12") square cake drum
127cm (50") x 1.5cm (½") width ribbon: peach
Non-toxic glue stick
Non-stick board and rolling pin
Ball tool
Blossom cutter: F2M (OP)
7 dowelling rods
Dresden tool
Drinking straw
Paintbrush: medium
Smoother
Small pieces food-grade foam sponge or kitchen towel for support
Small, sharp knife
Small spoon
Thin dowelling rod (e.g. barbeque skewer)

For the materials, equipment and instructions required to make Spud and Patch, see pages 54 to 57.

METHOD

Covering the cake drum and cake

1 Cut and fill the sponge cake with buttercream, then position the cake slightly towards the back of the cake drum. Cover the cake with a thin layer of buttercream.

2 Roll out 700g (1lb 9oz) of Flesh Sugar Dough on a non-stick board and cover the cake. Smooth over the top and sides with a smoother and cut away any excess paste from the base of the cake with a sharp knife.

3 Knead together the trimmings of Flesh Sugar Dough and roll out a long strip to fit all the way around the cake base. Cut a straight edge on one side of the strip, dampen the cake drum with cooled, boiled water and fix the strip to the cake drum. Cut to size and smooth down any joins, then trim away the excess paste from the edge of the cake drum using a sharp knife.

4 Dilute some Chestnut Paste Food Colour with cooled, boiled water or clear alcohol to make a colour wash. Brush this over the cake and cake drum randomly. Repeat the same process using Poinsettia Paste Food Colour.

Fencing

5 Add a small ball of Blue Sugar Dough to 250g (8¾oz) of White Sugar Dough and knead well to make a pale blue colour. Roll out and cut 13 fence posts measuring 6cm x 1.5cm (2½" x ½") and 18 fence panels measuring 9cm x 1.5cm (3½" x ½"). Attach the fence panels to the sides of the cake with edible glue, alternating and interlocking the panels. Secure

the fence posts to the ends of the fence panels.

Trough

6 Roll out 30g (1oz) of Brown Sugar Dough and cut out the following pieces: two panels for the front and back measuring 9cm x 2.5cm (3½" x 1"), two side panels measuring 4.5cm x 2.5cm (1¾" x 1"), a base measuring 9cm x 2.5cm (3½" x 1") and four square feet measuring 1.5cm (½"). Mark the panels with the blunt side of a small knife and assemble the pieces using edible glue. Secure to the front of the cake and leave to dry.

Stacked stones

7 Mix together 100g (3½oz) of White and 50g (1¾oz) of Maroon Sugar Dough, and mix 100g (3½oz) of Blue with 50g (¾oz) of White.

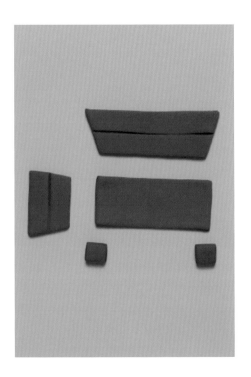

You will also need 250g (8¾oz) of Orange Sugar Dough. Push the three dowelling rods into the cake. Taking each colour in turn, roll and shape different sized stones and push them onto the dowelling rod, using orange, maroon and blue paste for the large, medium and small rods respectively. Build up each stack gradually, allowing the lower half to dry a little before stacking the top half (this prevents the lower stones from being squashed).

8 Stack three more piles of stones, one in each colour, on the cake drum. Reserve any remaining paste to build small stacks and pebbles after the cacti have been assembled.

Tall cacti

9 Push a 15cm (6") dowel into the cake between the two stacked towers at the back. Roll a tapered sausage shape from 45g (1½oz) of Green Sugar

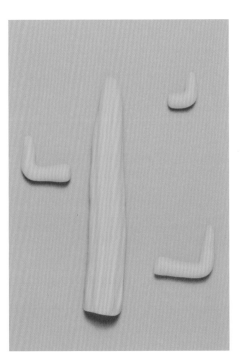

Dough, push this over the dowelling rod with the thinner end at the top and secure to the top of the cake. Run a Dresden tool up the main body of the cactus, working from the base to the top. Divide 5g (just under ¼oz) of Green Sugar Dough into three pieces for the arms of the cactus, shape and mark with a Dresden tool. Allow to firm, then attach to the main body of the cactus using edible glue. Repeat the same process for the two remaining cacti on top of the cake, varying the sizes slightly.

10 Make the cactus at the front of the cake in the same way using 85g (2¾oz) of Green Sugar Dough, but this time secure the base of the cactus to the cake drum and side of the cake.

Ball cacti

11 Divide the remaining Green Sugar Dough into different sized balls,

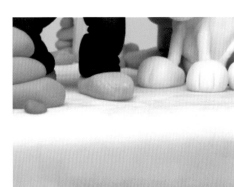

mark each one as before with the Dresden tool and attach to the cake drum in pairs and small groups.

12 Cut out several flowers from Red and White Sugar Dough using the blossom cutter (you will need more red than white). Attach the flowers to the tops of the cactus balls with edible glue. Roll tiny balls from the trimmings and secure one into the centre of each flower in the opposite colour.

Loose stones

13 Roll and shape pebbles and small stacks of stones from the reserved Sugar Dough. Secure to the cake drum with edible glue.

Patch

14 Make Patch following the instructions on pages 56 to 57 and secure him to one side of the cake top.

Stinky Spud

15 Follow the basic instructions for making Spud's head on page 54. For Stinky Spud, you will need to use Golden Bear Brown Sugar Dough for the head, feet, hands, gun and belt buckle and Black Sugar Dough for the body, arms and legs, belt, hat, holster and mask. You will need to allow each stage to firm, supported with pieces of foam sponge, to ensure the figure keeps its shape.

16 As Spud is standing up, make the feet first and work upwards. Attach the feet to the top front of the cake with edible glue. To make the trousers in a standing position, roll a tapered sausage from 25g (just over ¾oz) of Black Sugar Dough, bring the two ends together and cut to the same length. Mark with a Dresden tool and bend the legs into position. Secure to the feet and support with small pieces of foam sponge until dry.

17 Roll a pear shape of Black Sugar Dough for the body and model the base to fit on top of the trousers. Push a 20.5cm (8") length of thin dowelling rod through the body, down the left leg and into the cake, leaving 4cm (1½") exposed at the top to support the head later. Run the blunt edge of a small knife down the front of the body. Add the red and green scarf (see page 55) and bring the end to a point so that it looks like it is tucked into the shirt.

18 Make the belt and buckle from Black and Golden Bear Brown Sugar Dough (see pages 55 to 56) and secure to the waist with edible glue. Pinch a small ball of Black Sugar Dough, shape a gun handle and set aside. Knead the trimmings together and shape a holster, mark halfway down with a ball tool and attach to Spud's leg, just under the belt. Add a small ball of Golden Bear Brown Sugar Dough to the top of the holster and another to the base.

Roll seven tiny balls of Golden Bear Brown Sugar Dough and attach them around the top of the holster. Secure the prepared gun handle to the top of the holster with edible glue, holding it in place until it is secure.

19 To make the waistcoat, roll out 10g (¼oz) of Black Sugar Dough and cut a waistcoat to fit around the body. Round off the corners, secure in place and make two small rectangles for the front pockets.

20 Model the arms from Black Sugar Dough, bend at the elbow and mark creases with a Dresden tool. Secure both arms in position, supporting the left arm with foam sponge pieces and resting the right arm on top of the gun handle until the hands are prepared.

21 Model Spud's hands from Golden Bear Brown Sugar Dough (see page 55). Attach a hand at the end of each

sleeve with edible glue, resting the right hand between the top of the gun handle and the sleeve.

22 Secure the head over the dowelling rod and complete the face (see page 56). Do not attach the nose in place yet.

23 To make the mask, roll out 5g (just under ¼oz) of Black Sugar Dough and cut a thin strip to fit around Spud's head. Cut a mask shape with a small, sharp knife, make two eye holes using a drinking straw and attach the mask over Spud's eyes. Secure the strip around the back of the head, then attach the prepared nose into position with a little edible glue.

24 For the hat, roll out 25g (just over ¾oz) of Black Sugar Dough and cut out an 8cm (3") circle and a strip measuring 1cm x 13cm (¼" x 5"). Knead together the remaining Black

Sugar Dough and shape into a dome measuring 4cm (1½") at the base to fit centrally in the cut circle. Push the edge of your little finger into the top of the hat to make a groove, then secure the top of the hat to the brim and attach the strip around the hat. Fix the hat onto Spud's head with edible glue. Push the sides of the hat upwards and hold in place until firm.

To finish

25 Spoon some clear piping gel into the trough and drop small amounts on the top and down the sides of the trough. Drop small amounts onto the covered cake drum.

26 Secure the ribbon to the edge of the cake drum with a non-toxic glue stick.

Go West Mini Cake

Materials

15cm (6") round sponge cake
225g (8oz) buttercream
SK Sugar Dough: 3g ($^1/_8$oz) Brown, 300g (10½oz) Golden Bear Brown, 50g (1¾oz) Green, 25g (just over ¾oz) Red, 3g ($^1/_8$oz) White
SK Edible Glue
SK Edible Photograph
Icing sugar in a sugar shaker
Cooled, boiled water
White vegetable fat

Equipment

20.5cm (8") round cake drum
66cm (26") x 1.5cm (½") width ribbon: red
Non-toxic glue stick
Non-stick board and rolling pin
10cm (4") length of dowelling rod
Blossom cutter: F2M (OP)
Dresden tool
Paintbrush: medium
Small, sharp knife
Smoother
Sugar shaper

METHOD

Covering the cake and cake drum

1 Cut and fill the sponge cake with buttercream, position the cake off-centre on the cake drum and cover with a thin layer of buttercream.

2 Cover the cake with 300g (10½oz) of Golden Bear Brown Sugar Dough. Knead together the Sugar Dough trimmings and cover the cake drum.

Cacti

3 Make a sausage from 25g (just over ¾oz) of Green Sugar Dough and push this over a 10cm (4") length of dowelling rod. Model the side pieces and secure in place with edible glue.

4 Model several ball-shaped cacti and add red and white flowers (see instructions for the main cake). Attach to the cake drum and side of the cake with edible glue.

Pebbles

5 Roll several balls in various sizes from Brown Sugar Dough and place them onto the covered cake drum and cake.

Edible photograph

6 Cut the edible photograph to a 13cm (5") circle and apply to the top of the cake, following the instructions supplied with the photograph.

Rope

7 Soften the remaining Red Sugar Dough with a little white vegetable fat. Push the paste through a sugar shaper with a medium hole disc to create a long length of rope. Wind the rope around the edible photograph several times and secure in place with edible glue. Extrude another short length of paste and wrap this around the top of the rope to hide the ends.

To finish

8 Secure red ribbon to the edge of the cake drum using a non-toxic glue stick.

SPUD

Materials

SK Sugar Dough: pinch of Black, 10g (¼oz) Blue, 5g (just under ¼oz) Brown, 5g (just under ¼oz) Green*, 5g (just under ¼oz) Red*, 200g (7oz) White

SK Paste Food Colours: Chestnut, Jet Black, Lilac

SK Edible Glue

SK Edible Gold Paint

Cooled, boiled water or clear alcohol (e.g. gin or vodka)

Equipment

10cm (4") length of thin dowelling (e.g. barbeque skewer)

Ball tool

Dresden tool

Embroidery Grid Embosser (PC)

Paintbrushes: fine, medium

Small, sharp knife

*Optional extras for Stinky Spud and Christmas Spud

Note: There are two versions of Spud's colouring within the projects, so you will need to adjust the colour as required: use either White Sugar Dough painted with Chestnut Paste Food Colour (as described here), or simply use Golden Bear Brown Sugar Dough. The quantity of paste required is the same.

METHOD
Spud's head

1   Shape 60g (2oz) of White Sugar Dough into an oval and mark the mouth with a Dresden tool. Use the same tool to mark the lips and gathered fabric. Texture the Sugar Dough with the embroidery grid embosser to resemble sacking. Push the end of the Dresden tool into the head 1.5cm (½") above the mouth: the nose will be pushed into this hole later. Set aside to dry upside down so that the head holds its shape. The top of the head will be covered with a hat or hood, depending on the project, or the top part of the sacking will go on the top. To make this part, model a small disc of White Sugar Dough for the tie and shape a piece of Golden Bear Brown Sugar Dough (or White painted with Chestnut) for the sacking. Set both pieces aside to dry.

Trousers

2   Knead together 10g (¼oz) of Blue and 40g (1½oz) of White Sugar Dough and blend well to make a much lighter blue. Roll the paste into a pear shape and make a 5cm (2") incision from the thinner end for the legs. Smooth the cut edges and mark the trousers at the top of the legs and the knee area with a Dresden tool. Bend the top of the trousers over slightly to a sitting position.

Body

3   Add a small amount of Lilac Paste Food Colour to 60g (2oz) of White Sugar Dough and knead well. Divide the paste as follows: 40g (1½oz) for the main body and 10g (¼oz) for each arm. Shape the body into a pear shape, making sure that the base of this piece fits snugly in the top of the trousers. Roll a slim sausage for each arm and mark at the elbows with a Dresden tool. Secure to the shoulders with edible glue. Push a 10cm (4") length of thin dowelling down through the body from the neck to give support to the head (and hat).

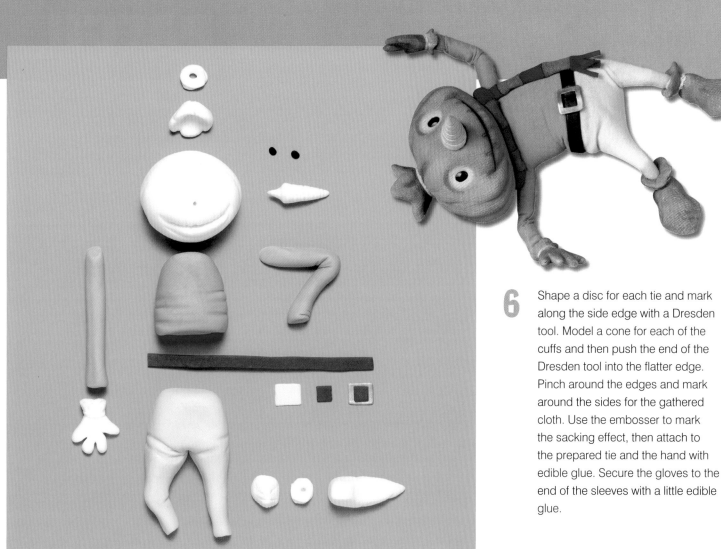

6

Shape a disc for each tie and mark along the side edge with a Dresden tool. Model a cone for each of the cuffs and then push the end of the Dresden tool into the flatter edge. Pinch around the edges and mark around the sides for the gathered cloth. Use the embosser to mark the sacking effect, then attach to the prepared tie and the hand with edible glue. Secure the gloves to the end of the sleeves with a little edible glue.

Feet

7

Divide 10g (¼oz) of White Sugar Dough in half. Prepare the ties and cuffs in the same way as for the hands, then shape the foot to a point and mark at the toes and the instep. Emboss as before and attach to the trousers with edible glue.

Belt

8

Roll out a small amount of White Sugar Dough, cut a 1.5cm (½")

Scarf (optional)

4

Colour the Green Sugar Dough with a touch of Jet Black Paste Food Colour to make a darker green. Divide the paste into several small balls of the same size and repeat with the Red Sugar Dough. Shape each ball into a square and attach alternately in a line with edible glue. Make small incisions at each end using a small, sharp knife to create a fringe. Attach to the neck with edible glue.

Gloves

5

For each glove, divide 5g (just under ¼oz) of White Sugar Dough into three balls: one small for the tie around the wrist, one medium for the cuff and one large for the main part of the hand. Model a disc for each hand and cut the thumb and fingers. Round off the cut edges with your fingers and thumb and mark the sacking over the hand with the embosser.

square for the buckle and set aside. Roll out 5g (just under ¼oz) of Brown Sugar Dough, cut into a strip 1cm (¼") wide and long enough to fit around Spud's body. Cut a small section for the centre of the buckle. Attach the belt to the body at the top of the trousers and glue the small square section for the buckle onto the prepared white square. Attach the buckle to the centre of the belt.

Spud's face

9 Push Spud's head over the dowelling rod and secure to the neck with edible glue. Shape 3g (⅛oz) of White Sugar Dough into a carrot shape and make a short point at the wide end. Mark with the blunt side of a small knife. Brush the nose hole with a little edible glue and push the short, pointed end of the nose into the nose hole. Hold the nose in place until it is secure.

10 Dilute a little Chestnut Paste Food Colour with cooled, boiled water or clear alcohol to make a light colour wash and brush this over the whole face using a medium paintbrush. Brush over the gloves and boots at the same time, but do not paint over the ties. Allow the first coat to dry, then apply a second coat, paying particular attention to the creases in the sacking to show definition. Add more paste colour to the mixture to make a darker brown colour and paint inside the mouth.

11 Make two thin, oval discs from small pieces of White Sugar Dough for the eyes and attach to the head on either side of the nose. Add two tiny Black Sugar Dough ovals for the centre of the eyes and attach with edible glue.

Finishing touches

12 Paint the underside of the shoes with diluted Jet Black Paste Food Colour.

13 Paint the buckle on the belt with edible gold paint using a fine paintbrush.

Materials

SK Sugar Dough: 3g (⅛oz) Black, 3g (⅛oz) Brown, 50g (1¾oz) White
SK Paste Food Colour: Berberis
SK Edible Glue
Dried spaghetti
White vegetable fat

Equipment

Dresden tool
Paintbrush: medium
Small, sharp knife

METHOD

Colouring the paste

1. Colour the White Sugar Dough with a touch of Berberis Paste Food Colour and knead well to make a cream colour.

Feet

2. Divide 20g (¾oz) of the cream coloured Sugar Dough into five equal pieces. Shape one piece into a tail, mark with a Dresden tool and bend the pointed end over slightly. Roll the other four pieces into pear shapes and mark three at the front with the blunt side of a small knife for the paws. Set aside. Shape a small piece of Brown Sugar Dough into a flat oval, attach to the front of the fourth paw with a little edible glue. Mark the paw like the others and set aside.

Legs

3. Roll two small balls of cream Sugar Dough into sausage shapes and cut to approximately 2cm (¾") long for the two front legs. Attach to the top of two cream feet. Set aside.

Body

4. Shape 20g (¾oz) of the cream Sugar Dough into a fat sausage shape. Flatten two ovals of Brown Sugar Dough for the patches and attach to the body with edible glue, one at the bottom, left-hand side and the other at the top, right-hand side.

5. Position the back feet at the base of the body with the patched foot on the right-hand side of the body and secure in place with edible glue. Add the tail between the back feet and the two front legs at the front of the body.

6. To help support the head, push a 5cm (2") length of dried spaghetti into the top of the body, leaving approximately 1.5cm (½") exposed at the top.

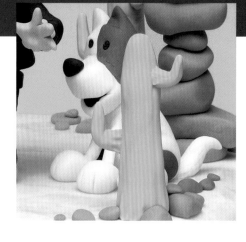

Head

7. Reserve a small ball of the cream Sugar Dough for one ear and pinch the same size ball of Brown Sugar Dough for the other ear. Shape the remaining cream Sugar Dough into an oval for the head, adding the last of the Brown Sugar Dough on the left-hand side at the top. Bend the oval slightly to form a muzzle. Mark the mouth with a Dresden tool and push a small amount of Black Sugar Dough inside the mouth. Gently push the head over the spaghetti at the neck and secure in place with edible glue.

8. Shape the two ears into triangular shapes and attach to the top of the head with edible glue.

9. Make two small eyes from Black Sugar Dough and attach to the front of the head. Roll the remaining paste into a ball for the nose and secure to the front of the muzzle with edible glue.

Cupcakes from Bobsville

METHOD

Sunflowers

1 Roll out 130g (4¾oz) of Green Sugar Dough on a non-stick board and cut out 13 circles using the large cutter from the set. Roll out 100g (3½oz) of Yellow Sugar Dough and cut out 13 flowers using a carnation cutter. Mark the petals with the blunt edge of a knife and secure into the centre of the green circles with edible glue. Roll out 50g (1¾oz) of Brown Sugar Dough, cut out 13 smaller circles for the centre and press into an embroidery grid embosser. Secure one into the centre of each flower.

Bones

2 Colour 40g (1½oz) of White Sugar Dough with Marigold Paste Food Colour, roll out on a non-stick board and cut four large circles using the cutter from the geometrical cutter set. Divide 20g (¾oz) of White Sugar Dough into four, roll each piece into a fat sausage shape and mark each end with a Dresden tool to make a bone shape. Bend each one slightly and secure to the coloured circles with edible glue.

Fish

3 Mix 40g (1½oz) of White Sugar Dough with 5g (just under ¼oz) of Blue Sugar Dough, roll out and cut out four large circles, as before. Roll out 15g (½oz) of White Sugar Dough and cut out four fish bones using the template. Secure to the light blue circles.

Materials

52 cupcakes
100g (3½oz) buttercream
SK Sugar Dough: 20g (¾oz) Black, 65g (2¼oz) Blue, 75g (2½oz) Brown, 30g (1oz) Flesh, 50g (1¾oz) Golden Bear Brown, 145g (5oz) Green, 30g (1oz) Orange, 100g (3½oz) Red, 280g (9¾oz) White, 150g (5¼oz) Yellow
SK Paste Food Colours: Marigold, Poinsettia
SK Food Colour Pen: Blackberry
SK Edible Glue
Icing sugar in a sugar shaker

Equipment

Gold cupcake cases
SK Clear Acrylic Cake Stand
Non-stick board and small rolling pin
Ball tool
Blossom cutter: F2M (OP)
Carnation cutter
Circle cutters (CT)
Dresden tool
Embroidery grid embosser (PC)
Geometrical cutter set (FMM)
Paintbrushes: fine, medium
Small, sharp knife
Smoother
Templates (see page 80)

TIP

These cupcakes are great for children's parties and can be presented instead of, or as well as, a larger celebration cake. If you need to alter the number of cupcakes, remember to adjust the quantities of buttercream and Sugar Dough accordingly – you should allow 10g (¼oz) of Sugar Dough per cupcake.

Fix it!

4 Roll out 10g (¼oz) of Orange Sugar Dough on a non-stick board, cut out a large circle and set aside to dry. Repeat to make a circle of Yellow Sugar Dough. When the paste is dry, write on the words *Fix it!* and *Yes we can!* using a Blackberry Food Colour Pen.

Footprints

5 Roll out 20g (¾oz) each of Marigold-coloured, Red and pale blue (White mixed with a touch of Blue) Sugar Dough. Cut out two large circles from each colour and set aside. Roll out 5g (just under ¼oz) of Brown Sugar Dough and cut two sets of paw prints using the circle cutter set. Secure onto the Marigold circles with edible glue. Roll out 5g (just under ¼oz) of Black Sugar Dough, cut two sets of paw prints slightly smaller than the previous set and secure to the tops of the light blue circles. Roll out 5g (just under ¼oz) of Yellow Sugar Dough and cut out two sets of bird footprints, using the template as a guide. Secure to the tops of the red circles with edible glue.

Sheriff badges

6 Roll out 40g (1½oz) of White Sugar Dough and cut out four circles as before. Knead together the

trimmings, roll out and cut rectangular nameplates for the centres of the sheriff badges. Roll out 20g (¾oz) of Red Sugar Dough and cut out two sheriff badges, using the template. Make two more badges in the same way using Blue Sugar Dough. Secure to the centre of the white circles using edible glue. Write the names on the nameplates with a Blackberry Food Colour Pen and attach to the centre of the badges with edible glue.

Warning signs

7 Roll out 20g (¾oz) of Red Sugar Dough and cut out two triangles using the template. Make two slightly smaller triangles from 15g (½oz) of White Sugar Dough and secure to the red triangles with edible glue. Set aside to dry. When the signs are dry, draw a 'Bob working' symbol, using a Blackberry Food Colour Pen.

Cacti

8 Roll out 40g (1½oz) of Golden Bear Brown Sugar Dough, cut out four large circles as before and set aside. Divide 15g (½oz) of Green Sugar Dough into two, roll out and cut two medium circles and two slightly smaller circles. Mark with a Dresden tool. Lay the smaller circles over the medium one and secure to the prepared larger circles using edible

glue. Roll out a little Red and White Sugar Dough, cut out four red and two white flowers using the blossom cutter and attach to the tops of the green circles. Pinch out tiny balls of each colour and attach to the insides of the flowers using edible glue. Divide the remaining Green Sugar Dough into two for the two tall cacti, take two small balls from each piece for the arms, shape and mark with a Dresden tool. Secure to the top of the two remaining Golden Bear Brown circles using edible glue.

Tools

9 Roll out 20g (¾oz) each of Brown, Yellow, Flesh, Blue and Orange Sugar Dough and cut out two hexagons in each colour using the template. Roll out 5g (just under ¼oz) of Red and a small amount of White Sugar Dough and cut out two traffic cones using the template. Attach the cones to the blue hexagons with edible glue. Roll out 15g (½oz) of Black Sugar Dough, cut out one of each tool shape and secure to the hexagons using edible glue.

Bob's head

10 Roll out 10g (¼oz) of Blue Sugar Dough, cut out a large circle and set aside. Mix 5g (just under ¼oz) of Flesh Sugar Dough with a touch of Poinsettia Paste Food Colour, divide into two and reserve half for Wendy's head. Pinch three small balls from the flesh colour for the nose and ears and set aside. Shape the remaining Flesh Sugar Dough into Bob's head, mark the mouth with a Dresden tool and secure to the large circle with edible glue. Roll a small ball into a pear shape for the nose and attach to the head. Push a ball tool into the two remaining balls for the ears attach to either side of the head with edible glue.

11 Divide a small ball of Brown Sugar Dough into four, shape and mark with a Dresden tool for the hair. Attach two pieces to the underside of each ear and two on top. Push a pinch of Black Sugar Dough into the mouth opening with a Dresden tool, and attach two tiny ovals of Black Sugar Dough in place for the eyes. Model the hard hat plus the brim and front section from 3g (⅛oz) of Yellow Sugar Dough (see the instructions for making Bob on pages 27 to 29.) Secure to the top of the head.

Wendy's head

12 Roll out 10g (¼oz) of Yellow Sugar Dough, cut out a large circle and set aside. Take the coloured Flesh Sugar Dough reserved from Bob's head, reserve three small balls for the nose and ears and shape the remaining paste into Wendy's head. Mark the mouth with a Dresden tool

and secure the head to the yellow circle using edible glue. Add the nose and ears in the same way as for Bob.

13 Shape small pieces of Yellow Sugar Dough into points for the hair and attach to the top of the head, marking with a Dresden tool. Make a hard hat from Blue Sugar Dough in the same way as for Bob and attach to the top of the head with edible glue. Add the mouth and eyes, as before, and secure in place. Roll two tiny balls of Red Sugar Dough for the earrings and attach one to each ear with edible glue.

Spud's head

14 Roll out 10g (¼oz) of Red Sugar Dough, cut out a large circle and set aside. Take 5g (just under ¼oz) of Golden Bear Brown Sugar Dough, reserve a small ball for the top of Spud's head and shape the rest into the head shape. Mark the mouth opening and creases with a Dresden tool and press an embroidery grid embosser gently into the paste to create a sacking effect. Secure to the red circle with edible glue.

15 Attach two ovals of White Sugar Dough for the eyes and add black pupils. Push a small amount of Black Sugar Dough into the mouth using a

Dresden tool. Mix a small ball of White Sugar Dough and with a tiny amount of Golden Bear Brown to make an off-white colour and divide in half. Shape one piece into a cone for the nose, mark lines across the top with the blunt edge of a small knife and attach to the face with edible glue. Shape the other piece to form the band at the top of his head, mark with a Dresden tool and secure in place. Shape the reserved ball of Golden Bear Brown Sugar Dough into the top of the sack, then use a Dresden tool to mark the creases and open up the top. Gently press the embroidery grid embosser to the top and secure over the band using edible glue.

To finish

16 Spread a little buttercream on top of each cake and carefully place the designs on the cakes, ensuring the buttercream holds them in place.

17 Display the cakes on an acrylic stand, or create your own centrepiece. Alternatively, you could place each cake in a small box as a party gift.

Spud's Halloween Pumpkin

Materials

2 x 20.5cm (8") round sponge cakes or 1 x 16.5cm (6½") spherical sponge cake
450g (1lb) buttercream
SK Sugar Dough: 150g (5¼oz) Black, 10g (¼oz) Blue, 60g (2oz) Brown, 600g (1lb 5¼oz) Green, 750g (1lb 10½oz) Orange, 200g (7oz) White
SK Paste Food Colours: Bulrush, Chestnut, Holly/Ivy, Jet Black, Lilac
SK Edible Paint: Gold
SK Edible Glue
Icing sugar in sugar shaker
Cooled, boiled water or clear alcohol
White vegetable fat

Equipment

30.5cm (12") round cake drum
100cm (39") x 1.5cm (½") width ribbon: orange
Non-toxic glue stick
Non-stick board and rolling pin
Ball tool
Dresden tool
Embroidery grid embosser (PC)
Paintbrushes: fine, medium
Small, sharp knife
Smoother

For the materials, equipment and instructions
required to make Spud, see pages 54 to 56.

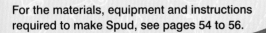

METHOD
Covering the cake drum

1 Knead 400g (14oz) of Green Sugar Dough and roll out on a non-stick board dusted with icing sugar. Dampen the cake drum with cooled, boiled water and cover with the Green Sugar Dough. Smooth over the top with a smoother and cut away the excess paste from the edge of the cake drum.

2 Randomly mark the paste with a ball tool to create a stippled effect. Dilute some Holly/Ivy Paste Food Colour with cooled, boiled water or clear alcohol and brush over the stippled area to create a shadow effect. Set aside to dry.

Pumpkin

3 Fill the centre of the sponge cakes with buttercream and stack one on top of the other. If you are using two round cakes, carve them into a sphere. Cut away a grooved dip at the centre of the top cake and then cut grooves down the sides from top to bottom to form a pumpkin shape.

4 Cover the shaped cake with a thin layer of buttercream. Knead 750g (1lb 10½oz) of Orange Sugar Dough, roll out and cover the whole cake. Smooth down the grooves with your hands and then use a smoother to create a crisp finish. Cut away any excess paste at the base of the cake and smooth down. Carefully pick up the cake and position it on the covered cake drum over the stippled area.

5 To make the stalk, shape 20g (¾oz) of Brown Sugar Dough into a cone and secure the pointed end into the dip in the top of the covered cake. Mark lines down the sides of the stalk with a Dresden tool and use the pointed end of the same tool to stipple the top of the stalk.

6 Make a colour wash by diluting Chestnut Paste Food Colour with cooled, boiled water or clear alcohol. Brush over the pumpkin, particularly in the grooves, at the base and at the top around the stem to give more definition to the cake shape.

7 Repeat the same process but this time using diluted Bulrush Paste Food Colour to define the base and top of the cake with darker shading.

8 To make the green stems, roll 150g (5¼oz) of Green Sugar Dough into four lengths, bringing one end of each piece to a tapered point and making the other end thicker. Curl each length in turn around the Dresden tool, brush a little edible glue on the thicker end and attach two to the base of the cake at the back and two at the base of the stem on top of the pumpkin.

9 Use the remaining 50g (1¾oz) of Green Sugar Dough to make different sized leaves. Push the blunt side of a small knife into the centre of each leaf from the base and attach to the curled stems with edible glue. Arrange the larger leaves at the top and the smaller ones at the ends.

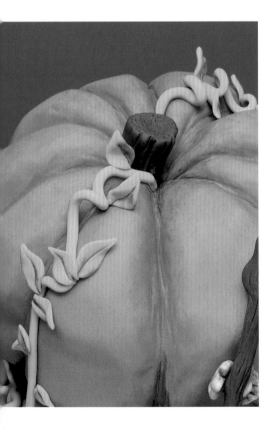

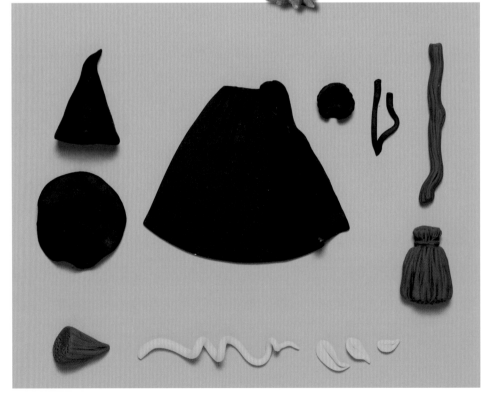

64

Broomstick

10 Divide 35g (1¼oz) of Brown Sugar Dough in half and roll one piece into a length for the broom handle, measuring approximately 13cm (5") long. Shape and mark with the Dresden tool, bend it slightly to give a crooked effect and set aside to dry.

11 Shape the other piece into the head of the broom and mark the bristles and the tie with a Dresden tool. Push the end of the Dresden tool into the centre of the bristles to support the handle. Secure the handle into the middle of the bristles with edible glue and set aside to dry.

Spud

12 Make Spud following the instructions on pages 54 to 56. (I made this model from White Sugar Dough painted with Chestnut colour wash, though you can make the model from Golden Bear Brown Sugar Dough to save time.) Do not attach the head yet.

13 To make the cloak, roll out 75g (2½oz) of Black Sugar Dough and cut out a rectangle. Gather along one edge and secure to the neck with edible glue. Roll out a strip of Black Sugar Dough and cut two ties to attach to the front of the cloak. Roll out a small disc from the trimmings and attach to the neck, on top of the ties.

14 Secure the head in position. Divide the remaining 75g (2½oz) of Black Sugar Dough in two. Shape one piece into a flat circle for the brim of the hat and the other piece into a tall, pointed cone with a bent tip for the top of the hat. Secure the cone to the brim of the hat, mark with a Dresden tool and the carefully secure to the top of Spud's head with edible glue.

15 Position Spud on the covered cake drum next to the pumpkin and secure in place with edible glue. Attach the broomstick to Spud's hand and the side of the pumpkin with edible glue.

To finish

16 Using a fine paintbrush and edible gold paint, randomly paint small stars over the cloak and hat. Allow to dry.

17 Secure the ribbon to the edge of the cake drum using a non-toxic glue stick.

Caught in a Snowball

Materials

2 x 20.5cm (8") round sponge cakes or 1 x 16.5cm (6½") spherical sponge cake

450g (1lb) buttercream

SK Sugar Dough: 25g (just over ¾oz) Black, pinch of Blue, 5g (just under ¼oz) Brown, 5g (just under ¼oz) Flesh, 1.3kg (2lb 13¾oz) White, 160g (5½oz) Yellow

SK Paste Food Colours: Poinsettia, Wisteria

SK Food Colour Pen: Blackberry

SK Edible Paint: Silver

SK Edible Glue

2 sugar sticks

Icing sugar in a sugar shaker

Cooled, boiled water or clear alcohol

White vegetable fat

Equipment

30.5cm (12") round cake drum

100cm (39") x 1.5cm (½") width ribbon: white

Non-toxic glue stick

Non-stick board and rolling pin

Ball tool

Circle cutters (CT)

Dresden tool

Paintbrushes: fine, medium

Small pieces food-grade foam sponge or kitchen towel for support

Small, sharp knife

Smoother

METHOD
Covering the cake drum

1 Knead 400g (14oz) of White Sugar Dough and roll out on a non-stick board dusted with icing sugar. Dampen the surface of the cake drum with a little cooled, boiled water and cover with the White Sugar Dough. Smooth the top with a smoother and cut away any excess paste from around the edge with a sharp knife. To make the surface look uneven, make several indentations in the paste using the end of a ball tool. Set aside to dry.

Covering the cake

2 Fill the sponge cakes with buttercream and stack one on top of the other. If you are using two round cakes, carve around the top and sides to form a ball. Cover with a thin layer of buttercream.

3 Roll out 700g (1lb 9oz) of White Sugar Dough on a non-stick board dusted with icing sugar. Cover the cake and smooth the surface with a smoother. Cut away the excess paste at the base of the cake and neaten with the smoother. Position

the covered cake towards the back of the cake drum, allowing enough room at the front for the characters.

4 To make the snowball look rough, push the ball tool into the surface of the paste, as before, and add additional small mounds of Sugar Dough.

Scoop

5 Roll out 150g (5¼oz) of Yellow Sugar Dough and cut the shapes that will form Scoop's front bucket, as follows: a 9cm x 4cm (3½" x 1½") rectangle for the bottom plate, a 9cm x 4.5cm (3½" x 1¾") rectangle for the top part of the scoop (leave this piece to dry over a rolling pin or curved former), a 4cm (1½") square for the face plate, a 9.5cm x 2cm (3¾" x ¾") rectangle for the top of the scoop (again, leave this piece to dry over a rolling pin or curved former), two rounded triangular sections measuring 2cm (¾") and two measuring 4cm (1½") at the

widest point for the side parts. Cut two medium and two slightly smaller discs using the circle cutters.

6 Knead together the Yellow Sugar Dough trimmings and roll out again, this time quite thinly. Cut six small discs using the smallest cutter in the set. Knead the remaining paste again and shape two connectors: they should be 1cm (¼") thick with a rounded top and curved base. The longest side of the connectors should be 2.5cm (1") and the shortest side 1.5cm (½") so they fit around the back of the curves on the top part of the scoop.

7 For the bolts, cut six small discs from a small piece of Black Sugar Dough and roll four small balls to go on top of four bolts (the two inside the scoop don't have the top part).

8 To make the eyes, roll out 10g (¼oz) of White Sugar Dough and cut two medium sized circles and two narrow crescent shapes. Attach the crescents to the edge of the circles

with edible glue to create the eyelids. Roll two small balls of Black Sugar Dough for the eyeballs and attach in place with edible glue.

9 Cut a wide mouth shape from White Sugar Dough. Draw on the markings with a Blackberry Food Colour Pen and then carefully paint around the markings with edible silver paint. Paint the eyelids and around the edges of the eyes and leave to dry.

Assembling Scoop

10 To assemble Scoop's face, secure the square section to the side of the cake with edible glue and attach the eyes and mouth.

11 To make the scoop, secure the flat base plate to the cake drum, squarely in front of Scoop's face. Add the two larger triangular sections to the ends of the base plate, then carefully attach the curved top part of the scoop to the back of the base plate and triangular sections. Support the

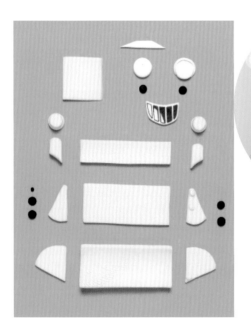

TIP

Scoop is easier to put together when the pieces are completely dry, so make the pieces a day in advance and allow to dry overnight before assembling them together.

scoop if necessary with pieces of foam sponge or rolled kitchen towel until it is held securely in place.

12 Attach the two smaller triangular sections to either end of the smaller, curved overlay for the top of the scoop and allow to dry completely.

13 Secure the curved sections to the back of the assembled scoop. Attach the small discs to the medium discs and attach to the back of the curved sections and the side of the cake with edible glue.

14 Position the prepared curved overlay of the scoop on top of the main section and secure to the outside at the halfway point with edible glue. Support between the sections with rolled kitchen towel until completely dry.

15 Add the small, yellow discs to either side of the scoop, one at the bottom of the main scoop and the other two on the top section at the middle and top. Secure two plain, small black

discs to the inside of the main scoop at the halfway point and two bolts on the outside of the scoop at the same point. Secure the last two bolts on the sides of the curved back supports with edible glue.

Zoomer

16 Roll out 60g (2oz) of Black Sugar Dough and cut two skis 1.5cm (½") wide by 6cm (2½") long. Shape the front of each ski to a rounded-off point, bend upwards slightly and leave to dry. Dilute a little Wisteria Paste Food Colour with cooled, boiled water or clear alcohol and paint the two sugar sticks. Set aside to dry.

17 Colour 80g (2¾oz) of White Sugar Dough with Wisteria Paste Food Colour and knead well. Shape the main front part of Zoomer, rounding off any sharp corners, and push your thumb into the Sugar Dough to form small arches on both sides of the body. Attach to the front of the

cake with edible glue and support it underneath with small pieces of foam sponge or rolled kitchen towel so that it is suspended 2cm (¾") above the cake drum.

18 Roll two small balls of Black Sugar Dough, push the end of each coloured sugar stick into the centre of each ball and attach the skis under the front of Zoomer with edible glue. Push each sugar stick into the arch of the main body, resting the ski on the cake drum. Secure the skis with a little edible glue if necessary.

19 Roll out 5g (just under ¼oz) of Black Sugar Dough and cut an arch for the top of Zoomer's face. Secure to the cake surface at the top of Zoomer's body. Roll two small sausage shapes for the front of Zoomer's body approximately 2.5cm (1") in length and secure in place. Roll out the remaining Black Sugar Dough, cut a mouth section and cut out the holes using a small, sharp knife. Secure to the front of Zoomer. Roll a sausage of Black Sugar Dough, flatten slightly, cut

to size and attach to the back plate to form a peak around Zoomer's face.

20 Divide 3g (¹/₈oz) of White Sugar Dough in half, shape two ovals and attach to the top part with edible glue. Roll the pupils from Black Sugar Dough and attach to the eyes.

21 To make the side flashes, thinly roll out a small amount of Yellow Sugar Dough. Cut a lightning flash (omitting the points) with a small, sharp knife and attach one on either side of the body with edible glue.

Bob

22 Shape a pinch of Blue Sugar Dough into a triangle and attach to the side of the cake to the right of Zoomer's head.

23 Reserve a pinch of Brown Sugar Dough for Bob's hair, then mix together 5g (just under ¼oz) of Brown and 5g (just under ¼oz) of White Sugar Dough to make a lighter brown. Divide in two and shape one piece into a fat sausage shape for the arm.

24 Cut a straight edge at one end for the wrist and cut the other end on the diagonal. Secure to the side of the cake to the right of the blue triangle. Roll out the remaining light brown paste and cut two 2cm (¾") squares for the front of the jacket. Fold one corner of each square back on itself to form an opening and secure to either side of the blue triangle.

25 Mix the remaining light brown paste with another 5g (just under ¼oz) of White Sugar Dough to make a much lighter brown. Divide in two and model the collar piece and a sleeve cuff. Shape and mark with a Dresden tool and attach the collar piece to the jacket opening and the cuff around the sleeve.

26 Use two thirds of the Flesh Sugar Dough for the front of Bob's face, a tiny piece for the ears and nose and use the remaining piece for the hand. Model the hand and the front part of the face, following the instructions on page 29. Attach the hand to the end of the sleeve and attach the face to the side of the cake above the blue triangle with edible glue. Add the

ears and nose, then use a little Brown Sugar Dough to make the hair over and just under Bob's ears. Attach a small amount of left over Black Sugar Dough into Bob's mouth opening and add two tiny oval shapes for the eyes.

27 Make the front section of Bob's hard hat from 3g (¹/₈oz) of Yellow Sugar Dough. Secure in place on the head with edible glue.

Assembly

28 To blend the machines and Bob into the snowball, roll small amounts of White Sugar Dough into sausage shapes, mark with a Dresden tool and secure them around the figures with edible glue. Smooth down any joins. Add pieces of White Sugar Dough over the machines and around Bob's collar, hat and arm, and mark as before.

29 Roll the remaining White Sugar Dough into small snowballs and attach to the cake drum around the base of the cake and the machines. Scatter some inside Scoop's bucket.

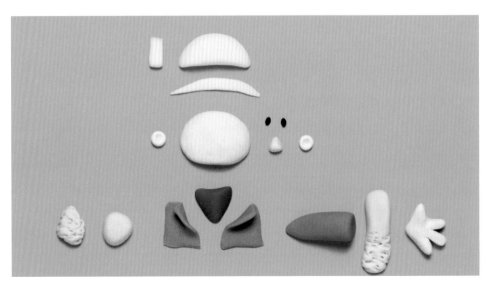

Wendy

30 Wendy on her skis is an optional extra, but looks great as she skis over the top of the snowball! Make the figure on a clear dowelling rod following the instructions opposite and push into the cake towards the back.

To finish

31 Secure a white ribbon to the edge of the cake drum with a non-toxic glue stick.

WENDY

Materials

SK Sugar Dough: pinch of Black, 5g (just under ¼oz) Blue, 10g (¼oz) Flesh, pinch of Red, 45g (1½oz) White, 10g (¼oz) Yellow
SK Paste Food Colours: Jet Black, Lilac, Poinsettia, Wisteria
SK Edible Glue
Cooled, boiled water or clear alcohol
Dried spaghetti
White vegetable fat

Equipment

Non-stick board and rolling pin
Ball tool
Clear plastic dowelling rod
Dresden tool
Paintbrush: medium
Small, sharp knife
Small pieces food-grade foam sponge for support
5cm (2") length of thin dowelling (e.g. barbeque skewer)

METHOD

Skis

1 Colour 10g (¼oz) of White Sugar Dough with Wisteria Paste Food Colour. Knead well, roll out and cut two strips measuring 1.5cm x 13cm (½" x 5"). Cut one end of each strip into a point, curve upwards and set aside to dry.

Poles

2 Break a piece of dried spaghetti into two lengths, each approximately 10cm (4") long. Mix together 10g (¼oz) of White and 5g (just under ¼oz) of Blue Sugar Dough to make a lighter blue. Break off four small balls and reserve the rest for the bodysuit. Roll two of the balls into small, flat discs and push a spaghetti stick through the centre of each one so that approximately 1.5cm (½') protrudes from the bottom. Secure in place with edible glue.

3 Roll the two remaining balls into small sausage shapes, push the other end of the spaghetti sticks into one end of the paste and smooth the paste down the spaghetti to form the handles on each pole. Dilute a little Jet Black Paste Food Colour with cooled, boiled water or clear alcohol and paint the exposed spaghetti. Set aside to dry.

Wendy's head

4 Add a touch of Poinsettia Paste Food Colour to the Flesh Sugar Dough to make it a little pinker in colour. Reserve three small balls for the ears and nose and two slightly larger pieces for the hands.

5 Roll the remaining Sugar Dough into an oval shape to form the head. Mark the mouth with a Dresden tool and gently mark under the bottom lip and at the sides of the mouth, up towards the nose area, with the flat side of the tool. Roll the nose into a pear shape and attach to the head with edible glue.

6 Turn the head upside down and set aside to dry. This will help the head to stay in shape and the flat area will be covered with Wendy's hair later.

Boots

7 Colour 10g (¼oz) of White Sugar Dough with Lilac Paste Food Colour and knead well. Reserve about a third of the paste to make the glasses, hair tie and side stripes, then divide the remaining paste in half for the boots. Model the boots, as shown, and attach one to each ski with edible glue.

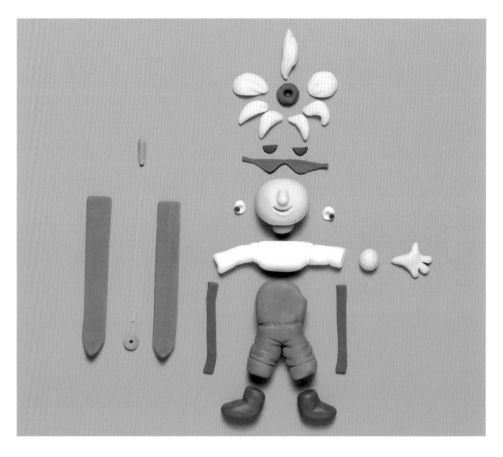

Bodysuit

8 Reserve a small ball of the light blue Sugar Dough for the collar and roll the remaining paste into a fat sausage for the body. Using a small, sharp knife, make a cut 2.5cm (1") up from the base to divide the legs. Smooth down the cut edges to round off the legs and mark the bodysuit with a Dresden tool to create the creases of her waistline, knees and turn-ups. Make an indent across the top of the bodysuit with the handle of the Dresden tool (this will support the white body/sleeves of the bodysuit), then flatten and square off the top edges with your finger and thumb.

9 To make the top of the bodysuit and sleeves, roll 10g (¼oz) of White Sugar Dough into a long sausage shape and taper the ends. Cut to size if necessary and attach into the groove at the top of the blue bodysuit. Mark creases in the sleeves with the Dresden tool and push the end of the tool into the end of each sleeve to make room for the hands later. Flatten the reserved ball of light blue paste into a disc for the collar and attach to the top of the bodysuit with a little edible glue.

10 Roll out half the reserved Lilac-coloured Sugar Dough and cut two strips to fit along each side of the bodysuit. Secure in place.

11 Carefully insert the clear dowelling rod into the base of Wendy's body and bring her legs slightly forward. Attach the legs to the boots with edible glue and set aside to dry, resting the dowelling rod at an angle until the body has set. When dry, it should look like the skis are coming forward and the body is slightly bent over.

Hands

12 Shape the two larger balls of coloured Flesh Sugar Dough reserved from earlier into hands. Use a small, sharp knife to make three fingers and a thumb. Smooth down the cut areas to round off the fingers and thumb. Mould the end of each hand to a point, brush a little edible glue into the end of each sleeve and push each hand into place, holding until secured into position. Brush a little edible glue in the palm of each hand, position a pole in each one and wrap the fingers and thumb around the handle tops. Rest the ski poles on small pieces of foam sponge to hold them at the correct height while drying.

13 Cut a 5cm (2") length of thin dowelling rod and insert through the collar of the bodysuit to give the head some support when attached.

Wendy's face

14 Turn the head the right way up and insert a small amount of Black Sugar Dough into the mouth opening

using the end of a Dresden tool. Gently push the head over the thin dowelling rod and secure to the collar with edible glue. Roll the two remaining small balls of Flesh Sugar Dough for the ears, push the end of a ball tool into each one and attach to the side of the head.

Glasses and earrings

15 Divide the remaining Lilac coloured Sugar Dough into two pieces, one for the glasses and the other for the hair tie. Roll out one piece and cut out the glasses using a small, sharp knife. Attach to the head over the top of the nose with edible glue.

16 Pinch two tiny balls from the Red Sugar Dough and attach to each ear for the earrings. Roll out the remaining paste and cut two lens shapes for the glasses. Attach in position with edible glue.

Hair

17 Model a small piece of the Yellow Sugar Dough into the ponytail shape and mark with a Dresden tool. Push a 2.5cm (1") length of

dried spaghetti into one end, leaving half exposed, and set aside. Build the hair up on Wendy's head in pointed sections, working from the back of the head towards the top, adding the fringe last. Mark each piece with a Dresden tool and attach with edible glue.

18 Roll the last piece of reserved Lilac Sugar Dough into a ball and mark with a Dresden tool for the hair tie. Secure to the back of the head with edible glue. Push the end of the Dresden tool into the centre of the tie, brush with a little edible glue and secure the ponytail into the middle by pushing the spaghetti into the head. Hold in place until firmly secured.

Spud's Secret Christmas Present Surprise!

METHOD

Covering the cake and cake drum

1 Cut and fill the sponge cake with buttercream and place the cake towards the front of the cake drum. Cover the whole cake with a thin layer of buttercream.

2 Mix together 50g (1¾oz) of Blue and 600g (1lb 5¼oz) of White Sugar Dough to make a light blue, roll out on a non-stick board and cover the cake. Smooth over the top and sides with a smoother and cut away any excess paste from the base of the cake with a sharp knife. Reserve the trimmings to make the parcels later.

3 Dampen the cake drum with a little cooled, boiled water. Roll out 200g (7oz) of Blue Sugar Dough into a long strip to fit all the way around the base of the cake, cut a straight edge along one side and fix to the cake drum with the cut edge against the cake base. Smooth over the surface with a smoother and cut away any excess paste from the edge of the cake drum with a small, sharp knife.

Christmas tree

4 Roll out 200g (7oz) of Green Sugar Dough and cut out one main piece and four sections of the Christmas tree using the templates. Set aside to dry, preferably overnight.

Materials

20.5cm (8") square sponge cake
450g (1lb) buttercream
SK Sugar Dough: 250g Blue, 150g (5¼oz) Golden Bear Brown, 300g (10½oz) Green, 80g (2¾oz) Orange, 250g (8¾oz) Red, 600g (1lb 5¼oz) White, 100g (3½oz) Yellow
SK Paste Food Colours: Chestnut, Daffodil, Lilac, Marigold, Wisteria
SK Food Colour Pen: Blackberry
SK Edible Paint: Gold
SK Edible Glue
Icing sugar in a sugar shaker
Cooled, boiled water
White vegetable fat

Equipment

30.5cm (12") square cake drum
127cm (50") x 1.5cm (½") width ribbon: blue
Non-toxic glue stick
Non-stick board and rolling pin
Ball tool
Dresden tool
Holly leaf cutter set (OP)
Paintbrushes: fine, medium
Small pair of scissors
Small, sharp knife
Smoother
Star cutters: set of 3 (FMM)
Sugar shaper with discs
Templates (see page 79)

For the materials, equipment and instructions required to make Spud, see pages 54 to 56.

5 When all pieces have dried enough to be handled, stand the main piece upright and support with small pots of food colour or similar to hold it in place. Attach the tree sections to the centre of this first piece using edible glue and support the sections in place, keeping them evenly spaced as before using small pots or similar. Leave to set for as long as possible, ideally overnight.

Garland

6 Soften 20g (¾oz) of Red Sugar Dough with a little white vegetable fat and push through a sugar shaper with a medium slit disc. Twist around gently and fix to the sides of the cake in 13cm (5") sections, using edible glue to secure the garland in place.

7 Roll out 20g (¾oz) of Green Sugar Dough and, using the holly leaf

cutter set, cut out 42 leaves. Mark each one down the centre with the blunt edge of a small, sharp knife and attach to the garland and corners of the cake base in groups of three or four with edible glue. Roll tiny balls of Red Sugar Dough for the berries and fix to the centre of each group of leaves.

Spud

8 Make Spud following the instructions on pages 54 to 56. Position the legs with the knees bent and secure the legs and body to the cake drum at the back of the cake. Do not make the arms yet and do not attach the head until after the cloak has been secured.

9 To make the cloak, roll out 100g (3½oz) of Red Sugar Dough and cut out the cloak following the template. Round off the corners and gather at the

shorter edge, then arrange the cloak around the back of Spud and attach at the neck using edible glue.

10 Secure Spud's head in position, then roll out 50g (1¾oz) of Red Sugar Dough, and cut out a semicircle 11.5cm (4½") in diameter. Gather at the straight edge to fit at the back of Spud's neck and attach to the cloak over Spud's

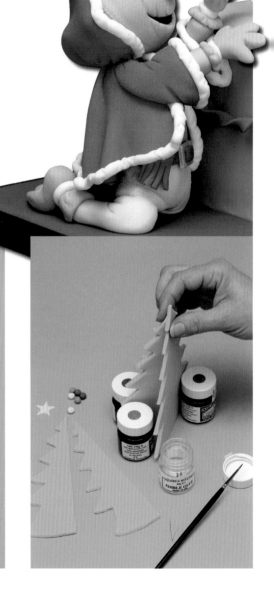

head, securing with edible glue. To make the white trim around the cloak and sleeves, roll 5g (just under ¼oz) of White Sugar Dough into long sausage shapes, mark with a Dresden tool and attach to the edges with edible glue.

11 Gather the Red Sugar Dough trimmings and shape two long triangles for the arms. Mark creases with a Dresden tool at the elbow and shoulder, then push the end of the Dresden tool into the wide end. Attach the arms to the cloak and add white trim, as before. Add the ends of the arms and the hands and secure in place, using the side of the cake for support.

Tree decorations

12 Secure the prepared Christmas tree towards the back of the cake top using edible glue. Soften 20g (¾oz) of White Sugar Dough with a little white vegetable fat and push through a sugar shaper fitted with a slit disc. Twist a long length of paste, then secure the end to the top of the tree at the back and bring it down and round the tree, attaching it to the points.

13 Using 5g (just under ¼oz) each of Yellow, Red and Blue Sugar Dough make small balls in each colour for the baubles and attach to the points of the tree using edible glue. Make the star with a small amount of Yellow Sugar Dough using the medium-sized cutter and attach to the top of the tree.

Presents

14 Take all the remnants of Sugar Dough and use them to make a present for each character. Make a crate for Spud using Golden Bear Brown Sugar Dough and mark the wooden panels with the blunt edge of a small knife. Model a cube for Wendy in White Sugar Dough and use diluted Daffodil and Chestnut Paste Food Colours to paint on the sunflowers. Make a cracker for Roley using Green Sugar Dough and cut a zigzag around the edge with a small pair of scissors. Make the colours for Zoomer and Trix by colouring White Sugar Dough with Wisteria Paste Food Colour and model two parcels. Shape a triangle of Red Sugar Dough for Muck's present and a green parcel for Travis. Model a bone for Scruffty from Marigold coloured paste and a blue bowl for Pilchard. To make Bob's parcel, roll out alternate sausage shapes of Red and Orange Sugar Dough, then cut and arrange them to make a checked pattern. Make the parcel shape from the trimmings, wrap the prepared paste around it, then smooth and shape the parcel with a smoother.

TIP
If the ribbon of paste breaks, just attach the loose end to the nearest point on the tree, cut off the broken piece and attach another length at the same point.

Bows

15 When making the bows for the presents, you can use either the same colour Sugar Dough as each present or a contrasting colour of your choice. To make a single bow, shape two small triangles, mark with a Dresden tool at one point and attach to the top of a present. For the ties (optional), roll two lengths of Sugar Dough, trim the ends, mark with a Dresden tool and secure to the present. Add a ball in the centre and mark with a Dresden tool.

16 To make a multiple bow, roll out a small amount of Sugar Dough and cut lengths several lengths 0.2cm (¹/₁₆") wide. Cut each length to 2cm (¾"), bring the ends together to form a loop and secure. Make around 10 to 14 loops for each bow, with a few smaller loops for the centre, and set aside to dry. Wrap two or four lengths of paste around the handle of a Dresden tool to form curls and set aside to dry. To assemble the bow, secure the long, curled lengths to the top of the present using edible glue, then attach each loop to the top of the present in a small circle, pushing the last three or four into the top of the circle to complete the bow.

Labels

17 Roll out 20g (¾oz) of White Sugar Dough and cut a label for each of the parcels with a small, sharp knife. Push the end of a paintbrush handle into the corner of each to make a small indentation and set aside to dry. Write the names on the labels using a Blackberry Food Colour Pen and attach to each parcel using edible glue.

To finish

18 Secure blue ribbon to the edge of the cake drum using a non-toxic glue stick.

Templates

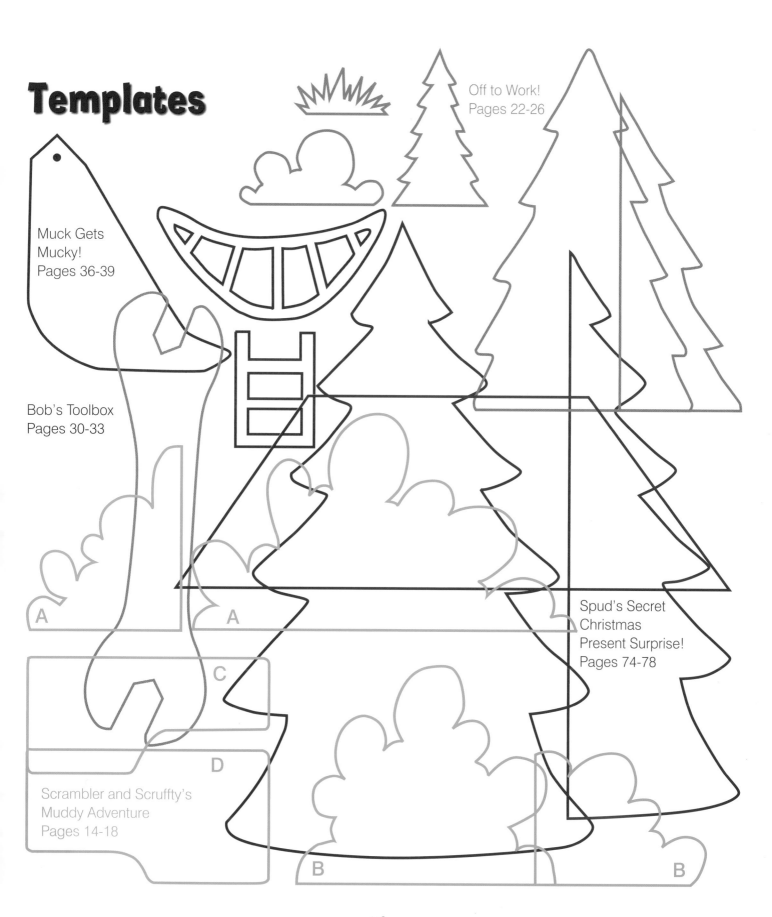

Off to Work!
Pages 22-26

Muck Gets
Mucky!
Pages 36-39

Bob's Toolbox
Pages 30-33

A

A

C

Spud's Secret
Christmas
Present Surprise!
Pages 74-78

D

Scrambler and Scruffty's
Muddy Adventure
Pages 14-18

B

B

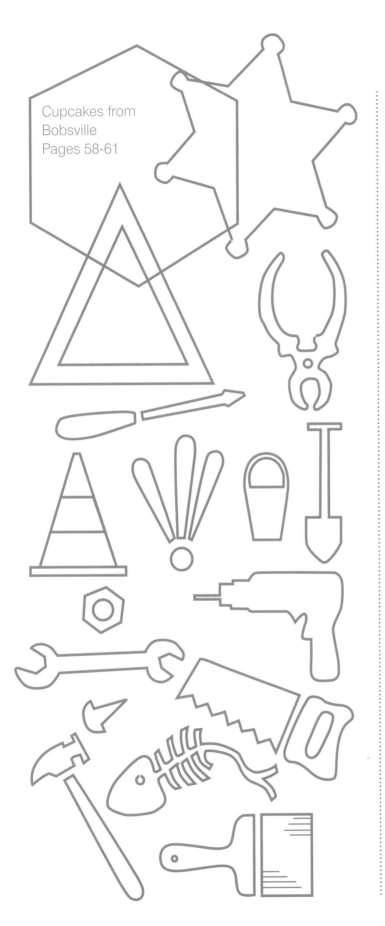

Cupcakes from
Bobsville
Pages 58-61

Suppliers

Cake Time (CT)
See Guy, Paul and Co. Ltd

FMM Sugarcraft (FMM)
Unit 5
Kings Park Industrial Estate
Primrose Hill
Kings Langley
Hertfordshire
WD4 8ST
Tel: +44 (0)1923 268 699
Email: clements@f-m-m.demon.co.uk
Website: www.fmmsugarcraft.com

Guy, Paul and Co. Ltd
Unit 10
The Business Centre
Corinium Industrial Estate
Raans Road
Amersham
Buckinghamshire
HP6 6FB
Tel: +44 (0)1494 432 121
Email: sales@guypaul.co.uk
Website: www.guypaul.co.uk

Orchard Products (OP)
51 Hallyburton Road
Hove
East Sussex
BN3 7GP
Tel: +44 (0)1273 419 418
Email: enquiries@orchardproducts.co.uk
Website: www.orchardproducts.co.uk

Patchwork Cutters (PC)
3 Raines Close
Greasby
Wirral
Merseyside
CH49 2QB
Tel: +44 (0)151 6785 053

**Squires Kitchen Sugarcraft
(SK)**
Squires House
3 Waverley Lane
Farnham
Surrey
GU9 8BB
Tel: 0845 22 55 67 1/2 (from UK)
+44 (0)1252 711 749 (from
overseas)
Email: info@squires-group.co.uk
Websites: www.squires-shop.com
and www.squires-group.co.uk